Santa Clara
County
Free Library

REFERENCE

COLORADO'S
FIRST PORTRAIT

Scenes by Early Artists

COLORADO'S FIRST PORTRAIT

Scenes by Early Artists

by

Clifford P. Westermeier

Albuquerque

UNIVERSITY OF NEW MEXICO PRESS

FOR THÉRÈSE

Endpapers: Front—"Bust," drawn by William M. Cary. (*The Aldine,* February 1873.) Back—The Gateway to the Garden of the Gods, drawn by Granville Perkins from photographs. (*Harper's Weekly,* July 19, 1879.)

Text © The University of New Mexico Press 1970. All rights reserved. Manufactured in the United States of America by the University of New Mexico Printing Plant, Albuquerque, New Mexico 87106. Library of Congress Catalog Card No. 72-99564. SNB 8263-0155-X. *First edition.*

PREFACE

As a result of the Louisiana Purchase, the eastern portion of Colorado became a part of the United States in 1803. Nearly 50 years passed before the western portion of Colorado was acquired by the United States. Claimed by both France and Spain, the area had been the home of prehistoric peoples and the hunting and battleground of the plains and mountain Indians. Spain hoped to solve the "northern mystery." France explored the land and French trappers sought wealth from furs. Previous to 1803 there was very little accurate information concerning the region.

Of the several explorers encouraged by President Jefferson to investigate the newly purchased territory, Zebulon M. Pike was the first to reach Colorado (1806). About a decade later Stephen H. Long brought back additional if not more accurate information than Pike concerning the geography, natural resources, flora, fauna, and Indians, both friendly and hostile. The reports of Pike's and Long's adventures and experiences presented such a depressing picture of the eastern plains of Colorado that the myth of "the Great American Desert" as a barren, windswept "no-man's land" was born.

In the years following, travelers and explorers went through the area in their journey westward. Among the travelers were Thomas J. Farnham, Dr. F. A. Wislizenus, Rufus B. Sage, Francis Parkman, George Ruxton, Lewis Garrard, Marcus Whitman, and William Gilpin. These men, in addition to John C. Frémont and other leaders of government and military expeditions, all either confirmed or discounted the earlier judgments and appraisals of Pike and Long.

Simultaneously, hunters, trappers, and traders—the fabulous mountain men —pushed into the pristine interior, probed the watercourses, crossed and re-crossed the ranges, and occasionally sought respite in the valleys and parks as they hunted the wilderness for beaver and other choice pelts. These men were the true pathfinders; others followed their trails to survey, map, and spread the story of the wonders of the great barrier between the desert and the lush valleys of the northwest and the future gold coast.

At this time, Mexico and her provinces north of the Rio Grande separated from Spain, and Americans welcomed the change in authority that permitted them to trade with Santa Fe and neighboring villages, Mexico's northernmost outposts. The "mountain branch" of the Santa Fe Trail followed the Arkansas River—the boundary between the two frontiers—westward into Colorado and south through Raton Pass to its final destination.

Bent's Fort, on the north bank of the river between La Junta and Las Animas, was one of the first and most notable trading posts in Colorado. In addition to Fort Pueblo and Le Doux's post near Florence, several other trading posts were established in the valley of the South Platte at Forts Lupton, Jackson, Vasquez, and St. Vrain which developed the Indian trade in buffalo robes. Forts Uncompahgre and Davy Crockett on the western slope were trading headquarters for the beaver trappers.

For nearly two decades, from the time of the ending of the fur trade to the beginning of the Civil War, Colorado remained a wilderness, the home of the mountain-dwelling Utes and several nomadic plains tribes. The trails north and south of the central massif provided access to the far west. Population was meager and, in the main, alien and savage, except in the small settlements in San Luis Valley. Colorado, apparently lacking agricultural and commercial opportunities, faced a bleak future.

Then came the gold rush of 1859. William Green Russell, an experienced miner from Georgia, had discovered gold in the Cherry Creek area in 1858, and there were rumors that the Pikes Peak region also had a "golden egg." Additional discoveries by Russell around Virginia Canyon, George A. Jackson's finds along Chicago Creek, John H. Gregory's rich lode in Clear Creek Canyon, and the Horsfal Lode at Gold Hill in Boulder County are but a few of the colorful events of that bonanza year. What threatened for a time to be a huge hoax became a dynamic movement. The trail west was jammed with eager throngs in search of gold, resulting in the first large settlement in the mountain region.

Mining camps mushroomed in the foothills and the gulches. Thousands of get-rich-quick hopefuls scoured and scarred the streams and hillsides. Thousands more hurried over the trails leading to the pot of gold. Behind the prospectors came the pioneer merchants and tradesmen with wagonloads of supplies and with only one aim—to mine the pockets of the miners. Within a year the Cherry Creek settlements had an air of permanency—systems of transportation and communication had been established, tent stores and log saloons did a brisk business, a banking house opened, and a school and a newspaper flourished.

Denver, the result of the merging of the Cherry Creek settlements, reflected the trend in the growth of Colorado towns and mining districts. As time passed, substantial buildings replaced the original crude structures and housed a variety of economic, social, cultural, and educational organizations and activities.

The phenomenal growth of the Pikes Peak communities soon brought demands from the frontiersmen for self-governing agencies, and early in 1861 led to the creation of Colorado Territory.

Between 1861 and 1870 Colorado faced several major problems, most serious of which were the Civil War and red-man/white-man clashes. Coloradoans, loyal to the federal government, promptly took measures to protect the isolated frontier of their territory. Indian depredations did much to consolidate this loyalty not only against the Indians but also against others such as the invading Texans who were defeated at Glorieta Pass before reaching the territory.

Colorado's participation in the Civil War was marred, however, by the Sand Creek Massacre in 1862, in which hundreds of Indian men, women, and children were killed while camped under the protection of military authorities. Two military engagements in 1868-69, resulting in the removal of the eastern tribesmen to reservations, ended this bloody chapter in the territory's history.

Additional problems of the 1860s included a mining slump, aggravated by rumors of mineral exhaustion and refractory ores, which, in part forecast the doom of the individual mine operator. These difficulties were surmounted, however, with the establishment of mining companies with enough capital to construct mills and smelters. The mountains continued to act as a barrier in transportation of supplies, equipment, fuel, and ore by wagon, but in the next decade this problem was also solved when a network of railroads was established.

During the early 1870s the railroad companies acted as advertising agents for colonization. Organized in the East the railroads promoted colonial ventures, stressed group settlement, and besieged prospective land buyers with an array of posters and leaflets about the rich agricultural lands available in Colorado. Many responded to these lures, and upon arrival in the promised land succumbed to the pressures of speculative townsite and land companies. Thus, a growing population and success in the agricultural venture paved the way for the next step—statehood. Disappointment, discouragement, and political wrangling dogged the Coloradoans in their plea for recognition which was finally achieved on August 1, 1876.

In the late 1870s silver became the state's leading mineral, especially after the discovery of the carbonate ores, rich in lead and silver, along California Gulch. From the abandoned gold sites sprang Leadville, the most fabulous of the silver camps. Sensational discoveries gave rise to more camps in this area, and in Aspen, Gunnison, and Creede. This boom intensified development in the mining industry and in transportation.

During the 1870s and 1880s the cattle industry was a natural outgrowth of the great demand for food on the mining frontier. The grasslands of the eastern plains fostered grazing and witnessed all the aspects of the developing range cattle industry. Within two decades, however, drouth, overstocking, blizzards, and the encroaching sodbusters drastically reduced this famed and fabulous industry which, toward the end of the century, was restricted to ranches. In addition to cattle, great flocks of sheep contributed to the phenomenal growth of the livestock industry.

Before the 1880s, knowledge of the region west of the Continental Divide had come only from the reports of the early explorers, trappers, and traders. Then, rather dramatically, the western slope came to the fore. Prospectors, land promoters, and town planners invaded the hunting grounds of the Utes and found them hostile. The Indians, disenchanted by the treaty arrangements to remove them from the desirable lands, became increasingly resentful. This state of affairs finally culminated in a conflict between the Indians and the troops—the ambush of Major T. T. Thornburg and the Meeker Massacre. Shortly after, the Indians were dispossessed, and western Colorado was thrown open for settlement.

Settlers rushed to the valleys beyond the divide, for on the plains east of the Rocky Mountains the success of the homesteaders in the river areas had demonstrated the feasibility of irrigation. Now, the agricultural frontiersmen dared to invade the high, arid, and treeless plains beyond the reach of the rivers. With them came barbed wire, windmills, and chill plows. Success was brief, for dry farming succeeds best in wet years, and the failures spelled out the need for better techniques. Plagued by grasshoppers, drouth, over production, a decline in prices, high interest, and freight rates, the farmers were in serious trouble.

They found aid and encouragement in farm, social, and financial-reform organizations—the Grange, the Greenback Party, and the Farmers' Alliances. During the 1890s they joined the miners in the Populist Party, which, as a champion of "free silver," won Colorado support. The Populist regime is one of the most colorful eras in the political history of the state, but the national election of 1896 struck the deathblow for "free silver."

Urbanization and further growth characterized the decade from 1880 to 1890. Colorado's natural resources—coal and iron—supported native industries —smelters, iron works, and the manufacture of mining machinery. Meanwhile the network of railroads helped to solve, in part, the problem of supply and demand, although the state was far from the major markets of the nation.

As a fitting finale for the waning century, a discovery in Cripple Creek touched off the last great gold rush in Colorado. Monetarily, it was the biggest and the best find and produced gold valued in 1899 at almost $20 million.

This picture history of nineteenth-century Colorado is limited to the woodcuts, lithographs, engravings, pencil and wash sketches, and reproductions of paintings produced during a bare fifty years of that century, from the decline of the fur trade to the so-called Gay Nineties. The selection of some 500 illustrations out of a collection of more than 2,000 imposed a difficult task on the editor-author. Regretfully, the artists and illustrators did not cover all the varied and significant aspects of this period in Colorado history; they did, however, capture the essence of the time.

The works of Paul Frenzeny, Jules Tavernier, Henry Worral, Theodore R. Davis, James F. Gookins, J. C. Beard, Thomas Moran, Albert Bierstadt, Frederic Remington, Rufus F. Zogbaum, and others enlivened the pages of the major periodicals of the nineteenth century: *Harper's Monthly, Harper's Weekly, Frank Leslie's Illustrated Newspaper, Cosmopolitan, Scribner's, Illustrated London News,* and others.

Less prominent names are found in innumerable publications—books on adventure and travel; personal narratives and reminiscences; promotional pamphlets on railroads, townsites, and resorts; as well as government and military reports and surveys.

Clifford P. Westermeier

CONTENTS

MOUNTAIN AND PLAIN

TUMBLING BROOKS, gently flowing streams, narrowing valleys, winding canyons, and high-walled gorges greeted the first intruders in the high country. Above the rocky walls towering snowy peaks beckon lovers of nature to worship at their shrines.

"King of the Mountains" (*Ovis canadensis*), the Rocky Mountain bighorn sheep, so called because of the massive spiral horns of the ram. Illustrated by J. C. Beard, famous animal artist, from a sculpture by R. A. Muller. (*Scribner's*, May 1881.)

A romantic and idyllic scene by Albert Bierstadt, probably from his western trip, 1859. (Richardson, 1867.)

The Snow Range or Snowy Range, so designated by most of the writers of early Denver, lies northwest of the capital city. (Dunn, 1886.)

A view of the Platte River Valley penetrating the foothills. (*Harper's,* June 1867.)

Rocky Mountain brook. (*Harper's,* August 1853.)

The Continental Divide—a very crooked backbone—runs roughly north to south through the center of Colorado. The highest peaks are not necessarily along the ridge. (Bishop, 1879-80.)

La Veta Pass—"the vein"—challenged by the Denver & Rio Grande Railroad in 1877. All extra cars were unhooked, and an extra locomotive added to climb an average grade of 211 feet per mile for 21½ miles. (Tenney, 1880.)

Sierra Blanca (shown), touted by the Denver & Rio Grande Railroad in 1891 as the highest peak in Colorado, actually is in fourth place (14,345 ft.).

An imaginary scene from James's trail looking north to the Snowy Range. (Crofutt, 1881.)

Pikes Peak from 40 miles northeast of the mountain. (Richardson, 1867.)

THE ROCKY MOUNTAINS were the first serious barrier for the frontiersman on his trek west. The cordillera, though it bears a single name, is not a single range. Rather it is made up of two **major** divisions—the Northern and Southern Rockies. The Southern Rockies begin in Colorado and split into the Front Range and the Back or Sawatch Range.

Alpine Lake as viewed by the Wheeler expedition through southern Colorado. (*Harper's,* May 1876.)

Two small lakes, named Chicago Lakes in honor of the city, are approximately 60 miles west of Denver. (Mathews, 1868-69.)

"Monarch of the Plains" (*Bos americanus*). Thousands of small bands, each led by a patriarchal bull, made up the original bison herds. Nomadic in habit, they roamed the plains, searching seasonal fresh range. Before 1850 the bison was indigenous in the area east of the Mississippi River; however, its principal home was on the grassy plains between the Missouri River and the Rocky Mountains. By 1875 two distinct herds emerged, northern and southern, and at one time they numbered approximately 30 million. (*Harper's*, January 1869.)

The bison or "Indian cattle" was the principal source of food and shelter for the western Indians. The meat was eaten fresh or cut into strips and dried for winter use—jerky (Sp. *charqui*). In particularly hard winters, as the food supply diminished, the Indians were forced to seek their prey. Today only a few protected herds are in existence. (*Harper's*, January 1869.)

Colorado has twenty-five varieties of cacti, ranging from the flat-lobed prickly pear to tree-like shapes in the southern part of the state. The various species are an important source of food for both man and beast. (*Harper's,* February 1868.)

Early in the 1870s buffalo slaughter reached a million a year. Professional hunters and sportsmen turned the plains into a veritable slaughterhouse—the beginning of the end of the nomadic life of the plains Indians. (Fossett, 1879.)

Buffalo grass (left) and grama grass (right), the forage of the plains. (Tenney, 1880.)

A tragic signpost of the plains. (*Harper's,* January 1869.)

Typical emigrant train observed by travelers crossing the plains before the coming of the railroad. (Fossett, 1876.)

A party of fifty-niners "at chores" as they settle down for an evening meal in their camp on the plains. (*Miners' Hand-Book,* 1859.)

Scarcity of water in river beds often necessitated digging for it. (Drake, 1887.)

A storm on the plains, sketched by J. F. Gookins. One of eight illustrations resulting from his trip with an emigrant train to Denver. (*Harper's Weekly,* October 13, 1866.)

Crouching around a campfire—as women and children prepare for bed, and horses graze nearby—the men relax, smoke, recount the events of the day, and ponder the future. "Emigrants on Their Way Southwest" by Thomas Moran. (*Illustrated London News.* August 15, 1885.)

"Evening on the Plains" by W. H. Gibson depicts preparation of a meal, while draft-oxen graze in the distance. Strips of flesh, hung out like a washing, are being dried to provide jerky for the lean times to come. (Ingersoll, 1883.)

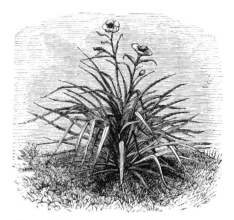

Yucca filamentosa, popularly called soapweed or Spanish bayonet, is found on the eastern prairies and in the western mesa country. Indians used the fiber for ropes, the ground pods for flour, and the roots mixed with water to form a soapy lather. (*Harper's,* July 1867.)

The bullwagon, with the bullwhacker in charge, carried freight to the settlements along the Front Range. One can imagine the blasphemous and colorful words of the driver as he prods the sluggish animals. (Manning, 1876.)

DWELLERS OF THE CLIFFS

THE HISTORIAN must rely on anthropological and archaeological findings for information concerning early man in Colorado. Although no skeletal remains of man were found, two types of stone artifacts of the vanished people were discovered.

The Folsom Points, first found near Folsom, New Mexico, and later in various parts of Colorado, were fashioned by skilled hands and used as weapons in hunting prehistoric bison.

Furthermore, the discovery of stone weapons in Yuma County, Colorado, again verifies the presence of primitive man in that area. What is known of these earliest inhabitants can only come from studying their tools, weapons, and the bones of the slain animals.

The people who followed them—the Basket Makers and the Cliff Dwellers—had no cultural relationship with the earlier inhabitants; but evidence of their activities on the mesa tops and in the caves of the walls of the canyons enlarges our knowledge considerably.

Cliff dwellings in southwestern Colorado. (Crofutt, 1881.)

THE SANDSTONE WALLS of the canyon valleys in southwestern Colorado have varying degrees of hardness. Erosion of softer layers created caverns which invited the Cliff Dwellers to build houses. Some caves permitted the construction of only one or two buildings; large caverns accommodated several, forming a community with kivas, granaries, and protective front walls.

Cliff Dwellers often constructed a circular watch tower on top of the mesa and surrounding heights with ladder access to it and their walled-up caverns on the face of the cliffs. (Denver & Rio Grande Railroad, 1891.)

A section of a cliff showing two-story houses, 700 feet above the Mancos River. (*Scribner's*, December 1878.)

Father Escalante, a Spanish priest, was the first European to see these ruins. In search of a route from Mexico to California in 1776, he came across the Mancos River and designated the region as Mesa Verde. (*Lippincott's,* November 1880.)

Spruce Tree House from across the canyon of the same name. It is one of the largest ruins in Mesa Verde National Park—a village in itself—with an estimated population of 200 inhabitants at one time. (*Harper's,* September 1896.)

An artist's impression of a Spanish missionary's first view of the San Juan Valley in 1540. Historical evidence does not support the presence of the Spanish in Colorado at this early date. (Crofutt, 1881.)

Signature of Captain Don Juan de Ulibarri. (Twitchell, 1914.)

Signature of Colonel Don Pedro de Villasur. (Twitchell, 1914.)

TRAILBLAZERS

RUNAWAY INDIANS from New Mexican settlements led the first recorded Spanish expeditions into Colorado Territory. Juan Archuleta brought back the Indians who had fled New Mexico in 1650, from El Quartelejo, a region east of Pueblo.

In 1706, Juan Ulibarri, also for the purpose of returning runaway Indians, led an expedition into eastern Colorado. At the same time he took note of the position of the French and observed their influence among the plains tribesmen. Furthermore, he took formal possession of the region in the name of King Philip V.

In the early 1700s the encroachment of French traders and trappers caused concern to the Spanish whose prestige among the Indians began to decline. To check the French intruders, Spanish authorities sent expeditions northward into Colorado. In 1720, Pedro de Villasur and his party followed the South Platte into Nebraska, where, on August 13, near North Platte, the Pawnees, probably encouraged by the French, launched an attack which stalled Spanish efforts to occupy eastern Colorado. In 1763, at the conclusion of the French and Indian War, the rivalry for Colorado came to an end when France ceded her claims west of the Mississippi to Spain.

Shortly thereafter, threats of English and Russian expansion along the Pacific Coast caused the Spanish to establish missions and settlements in California. By 1776, Spain realized that these outposts should be tied to the settlements in New Mexico. The Dominguez-Escalante expedition set out to open the overland route but failed to do so; however, the chronicle of Escalante records the first detailed information concerning large areas of western Colorado.

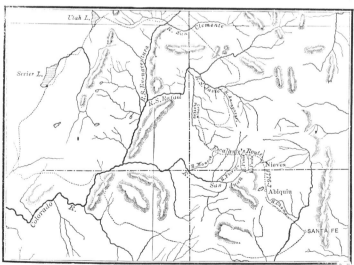

Escalante's route through Colorado. (Bancroft, 1890.)

IN 1806, LIEUTENANT ZEBULON M. PIKE was officially comissioned to find the headwaters of the Arkansas and Red rivers, to collect specimens of the natural resources, and to make scientific observations. He and his party suffered extreme hardships and were finally captured by the Spanish in the San Luis Valley, taken to Santa Fe, then to Chihuahua, Mexico, before being permitted to return to the United States in the summer of 1807.

Zebulon M. Pike (1779-1813), discoverer of the peak which bears his name. Although his records were confiscated, he was able to reconstruct his notes and prepare them for publication, which added to knowledge of Colorado and the Southwest. (Miles, 1896.)

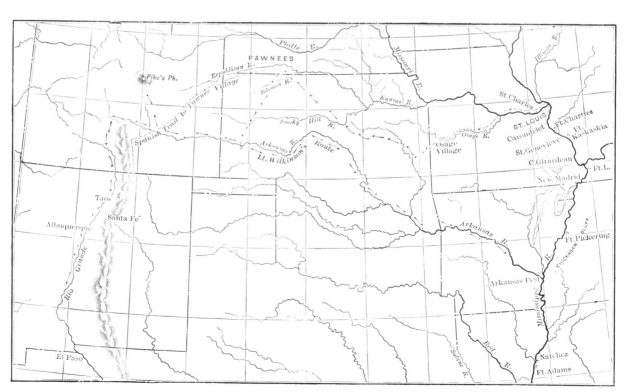

A map illustrating Pike's explorations west of the Mississippi and a portion of his captors' route. (Drake, 1887.)

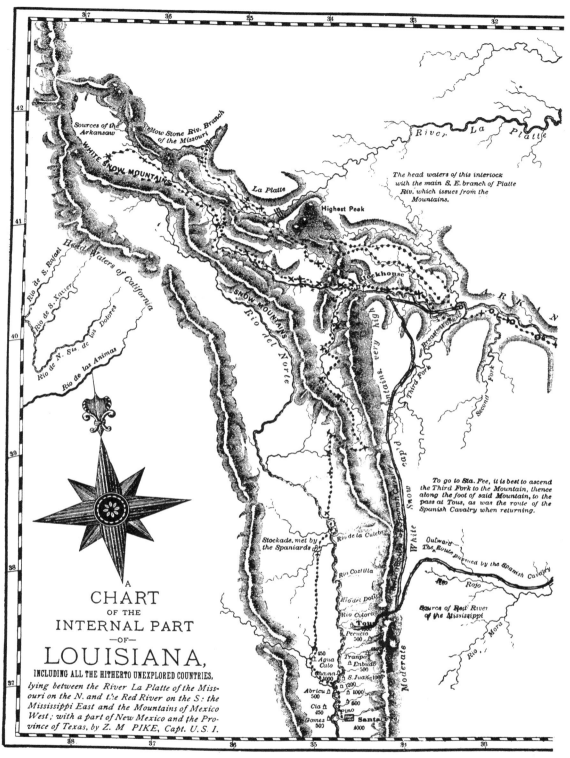

Western portion of Pike's map indicating his wanderings in the mountains of southern Colorado. The crosses mark his camps; the circles along the Arkansas River mark the camps of the Spanish cavalry. (Smiley, 1903.)

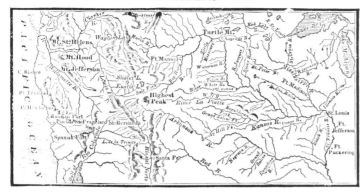

Rector's map of 1818. Of particular interest is the designation of the "Highest Peak." (Bancroft, 1890.)

A view of Longs Peak from the Cache la Poudre Canyon. (Crofutt, 1881.)

Stephen H. Long, the explorer, found neither the Red River nor the headwaters of the South Platte. Both Long and Pike describe the plains as a desert country unsuitable for agriculture. (Drake, 1887.)

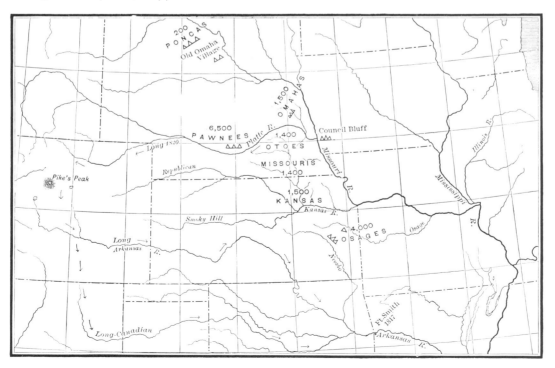

FORTS AND POSTS

Your sincere friend C. Carson

Kit Carson, the most famous of mountain men, is the classic personification of the virile and valorous West. (*Harper's*, September 1862.)

MEXICO, after its independence from Spain in 1821, welcomed American trade over the recently established Santa Fe Trail. Taos and Santa Fe were the bases of operations for trappers and traders in southern Colorado. In the northwest, Fort Davy Crockett was established at Brown's Hole on the Green River and Fort Uncompahgre on the Gunnison in the western part of the state.

Because beaver, long the prize fur for trappers, was becoming scarce and the market for beaver pelts had been ruined by the fashion for silk hats, many mountain men began to engage in the buffalo robe trade, which led to the establishment of posts where the Indians traded the dressed hides of buffaloes for other goods.

The old adobe fort at Pueblo overlooking the Arkansas River. Before the trading post was established in 1842, the site had been frequented by early Spanish and American explorers and by trappers and traders of various nationalities. (*Lippincott's*, December 1880.)

Bent's Fort, an adobe structure, measured about 135 by 180 feet. It consisted of a central court, two circular bastions, and an adobe-walled cattle corral. (Abert, 1845.)

Ceran St. Vrain, reputedly a descendant of a French nobleman, in partnership with Charles and William Bent, built Fort St. Vrain (c. 1838), the largest trading post on the South Platte. (Conard, 1890.)

Bent's Fort was ideally located for trade with implacable enemies—the Arapahoes and Cheyennes north of the river, and the Comanches and Kiowas to the south. After 1840, peace between these tribesmen eased the situation and improved trading conditions.

Fort St. Vrain. (Smiley, 1903.)

Fort St. Vrain, abandoned in 1844, was first known as Fort Lookout, located halfway between Bent's Fort and Fort Laramie on the North Platte to serve the northern Cheyennes and the Sioux. The volume of trade was not sufficient to support the posts—Forts Lupton, Jackson, and Vasquez—which dotted the South Platte Valley.

This structure is identified by Margaret Long, *The Overland Trail,* as a sketch of Fort Vasquez built in 1838. However, this illustration is used to depict other buildings associated with early Colorado history. (*Scribner's,* August, 1876.)

Artist Alfred R. Waud vividly records the wretched conditions of a forced march led by Captain R. B. Marcy from Fort Bridger, Utah, to Fort Union, New Mexico, on their arrival in 1858 at Fort Massachusetts, Colorado Territory. (*Harper's,* September 1866.)

Fort Massachusetts as sketched by Richard H. Kern. The first United States military post in Colorado, it was built in 1852 on Ute Creek near the base of Mount Blanca (an area then part of New Mexico but later allocated to Colorado). (Beckwith, 1855.)

In 1858, Fort Garland replaced Fort Massachusetts and guarded the route of the Sangre de Cristo Pass, six miles southward. The one-story adobe buildings enclosed a quadrangle parade ground and accommodated two companies. Restored, the fort is now the property of the Colorado State Historical Society.

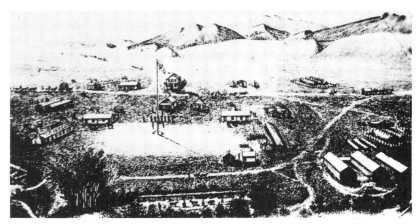

Old Fort Collins, 1865, originally Camp Collins. It was established to protect the ranchers and farmers in the Cache la Poudre Valley and to guard the Overland Trail from Indian depredations. Copyright 1899 by M. D. Houghton. (Western Collection, Colorado State Historical Society.)

A sketch by T. Nave depicting the battle of June 7, 1865, at Fort Garland. (Western Collection, Colorado State Historical Society.)

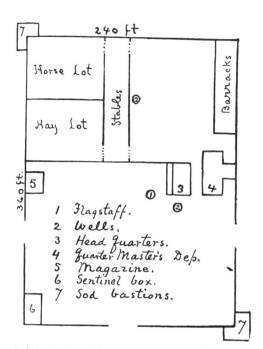

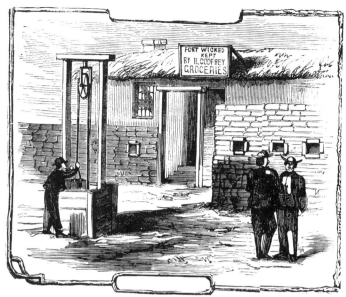

"Fort Wicked," a ranch and station on the Overland Trail, near present Merino. Holon Godfrey, a station master, and three other men held off a force of Cheyennes in January 1865. Godfrey acquired, thereafter, the reputation of "Old Wicked." (*Harper's Weekly,* October 13, 1866.)

Original plan of Fort Sedgwick. (Ware, 1911.)

"Fort Sedgwick, C. T.," built in 1864 and named for General John Sedgwick of the Union Army. It served as a fort until 1871 when the Indians of northeastern Colorado were subdued. (Western Collection, Colorado State Historical Society.)

James P. Beckwourth—mulatto trader, one-time war chief of the Crow, teller of tall tales, and founder of Pueblo—dressed in the hunter's costume. (Beckwourth, 1856.)

THE FUR TRAPPERS AND TRADERS—fearless, rugged men with rifles, traps, and a mount or two—accepted a perilous, lonesome life on the frontier.

After collecting the catch, they skinned, scraped, and smoked the pelts which were added to the pack. Trapping took place in the fall and spring. The highlight of the summer was the rendezvous to which they brought their catch in exchange for new outfits, trinkets for their Indian wives, a few luxuries from civilization, and always whiskey.

They were "a reckless breed of men" but truly a band to whom the nation owes much.

Jim Baker, skilled frontiersman, in hand-to-hand combat with a "varmint." (*Harper's,* September 1866.)

In the early 1850s, Joseph B. Doyle, Dick Wootton, and others established ranches near the mouths of the Huerfano and St. Charles rivers in the Arkansas Valley. Indian attacks forced their abandonment by 1855. (Conard, 1890.)

"Uncle Dick" Wootton, fabulous figure of the mountain frontier—trapper, scout, trader, freighter, herder, and businessman—built a road over Raton Pass and collected tolls, often at gunpoint. (Conard, 1890.)

A buffalo robe press, an essential piece of equipment in the buffalo robe trade. (*Harper's,* January 1869.)

By the early 1840s, most of the posts had been deserted; however, Bent's Fort in 1846 accommodated General Stephen W. Kearny's Army of the West on its march to Santa Fe, New Mexico.

The Catholic church at Guadalupe. This settlement was abandoned because of threatening floods from the Conejos River. (*Harper's*, May 1876.)

Lucien B. Maxwell, western trader and scout, fell heir to a land grant of approximately 1,700,000 acres in New Mexico and Colorado, given to Guadalupe Miranda and Charles Beaubien. Maxwell sold it to a British syndicate for more than $1 million. (Conard, 1890.)

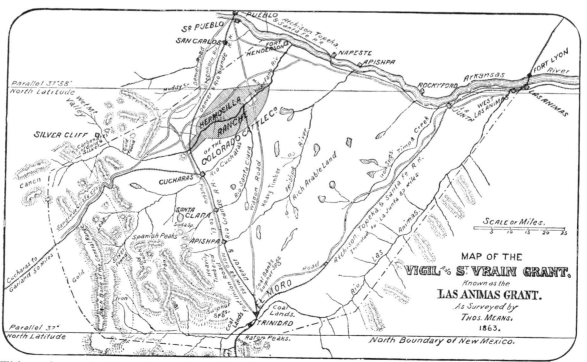

Title to thousands of acres in southern Colorado may be traced to the land grants made in the early 1840s by the Mexican government to promote settlement on its frontier. After the Mexican War the United States confirmed some of the titles and denied others. (Fossett, 1879.)

The original Salazar store in San Luis, an 1851 settlement which claims to be the oldest in Colorado. (Western Collection, Colorado State Historical Society.)

When the Denver & Rio Grande Railroad built south from Alamosa, it established Antonito near Conejos. Antonito became an important shipping center for cattle. (*Leslie's,* May 28, 1881.)

View of town of Conejos where the first Catholic church in Colorado, "Our Lady of Guadalupe," was built in 1854. (*Harper's,* May 1876.)

RED MAN
VS.
WHITE MAN

THE MOUNTAIN-DWELLING UTES were considered the only tribe indigenous to Colorado. Grouped in four major divisions—Southern, White River, Tabeguache, and Uintah Ute—they held the mountain region. As enemies of the plains tribes, the Cheyennes and Arapahoes, they guarded the low passes from intrusion. The Utes were never really conquered.

Ute squaws and papooses. (*Leslie's*, November 15, 1879.)

Squaws and the interior of a Ute wickiup. (Ingersoll, 1883.)

Chief Unca of the White River Utes. (*Harper's Weekly,* October 25, 1879.)

Chief Conniach. (*Leslie's,* September 3, 1879.)

Chiefs of the Uncompahgre Utes. (Wood, 1889.)

Southern Ute braves. (*Harper's,* May 1876.)

Typical Indian encampment along the Front Range of the mountains. (*Harper's,* March 1880.)

Braves making arrows. Sketched by William Cary, a prolific illustrator of the western scene. (*Scribner's,* December 1871.)

A craterlike area on the plains served as protection while standing off the Cheyennes. (Dunn, 1886.)

Chiefs of the Cheyenne and Arapahoe tribes, among them Little Raven (portrayed) and Black Kettle, negotiated the Treaty of Fort Wise in 1861. The cession of land to placate the demands of gold seekers neither pleased the Indians nor solved their problems. (Dunn, 1886.)

This engraving of George Bent (son of William) shows the Indian features inherited from his mother, Owl Woman, a member of the Cheyenne tribe. (Dunn, 1886.)

Camp Weld, Colorado Territory—site of the Indian council of September 28, 1864. Here Governor John Evans, Major Edward, Colonel John Chivington, and others met with Cheyenne Chief Neva and Arapahoe chiefs Bull Bear, Black Kettle, and One Eye. (Western Collection, Colorado State Historical Society.)

Indian attacks on stagecoaches, often the only lines of communication and transportation, between Fort Morgan and Julesburg in midsummer of 1864 crystallized the hostility of the settlers against the Indians. (Dunn, 1886.)

Black Kettle, Chief of the Cheyennes. (Western Collection, Colorado State Historical Society.)

DURING THE EARLY YEARS of the Civil War, relationships between red man and white man steadily deteriorated because the Indian sensed the weak position of the white man.

In the spring of 1864 tension mounted when Indians murdered the Hungate family on their ranch within 30 miles of Denver. Coloradoans feared a general Indian uprising.

In late September, Governor John Evans held a grand council at Camp Weld with Arapahoe and Cheyenne chiefs who insisted that they desired peace but could not control their warriors nor their war parties. Since a state of war existed, the chiefs left without a peace treaty.

At first the governor's policy vacillated between peace and war, but later he leaned toward a military solution. Late in November, Colonel John M. Chivington, the Fighting Parson and hero of Glorieta Pass, led about one thousand troops to the Arapahoe and Cheyenne Sand Creek reservation. At dawn they attacked the sleeping Indian village with guns, knives, and sabers. Not until some five hundred men, women, and children lay dead and mutilated did the attack cease. The Sand Creek Massacre is considered the blackest blot on Colorado history and is still the subject of much discussion and heated argument.

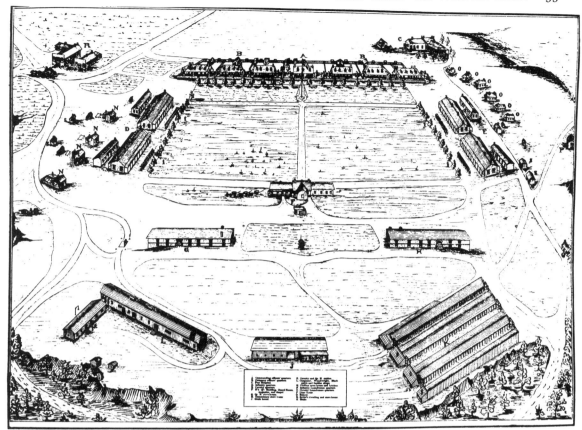

From Fort Lyon on November 29, 1864, Colonel Chivington and his cavalry marched against Black Kettle's sleeping village on Sand Creek. (Barnes, 1875.)

The charge on Black Kettle's camp—the infamous Sand Creek Massacre. (Dunn, 1886.)

Following the Sand Creek Massacre, the Indians continued their forays into Colorado Territory. Artist Rufus F. Zogbaum depicts the defiance of Roman Nose, the great Cheyenne war chief, at the Battle of Beecher Island, 1868. (*Harper's*, June 1895.)

A sketch of Colonel George A. Forsyth and fifty scouts pinned down on the low sandy island in the Arickaree River. (*Harper's*, June 1895.)

The first day of battle claimed the life of Lt. Fred Beecher, for whom the island is named, and left Colonel Forsyth severely injured. During one of the many charges Chief Roman Nose also was slain. The Indians, who were repelled by the besieged men, nevertheless continued to shower them with arrows and bullets. Two scouts managed to escape and bring relief troops from Fort Wallace, Kansas. (*Scribner's,* November, 1901.)

One thousand Indians continued the siege for nine days. The bodies of slain horses, after edible portions had been removed, served as breastworks. (Ellis, 1892.)

A mounted warrior attacking a cavalryman on foot. (Indian Sketchbook, Western Collection, Colorado State Historical Society.)

Indians pursued by scouts and troopers. (Indian Sketchbook, Western Collection, Colorado State Historical Society.)

Another rush, created by the discovery of gold and silver in the San Juan Mountains, violated the treaty with the Utes. The prospectors' invasion of the Ute reservations in the late 1870s and 1880s led to trouble and a reversal of the Indians' friendly attitude. (*Harper's Weekly*, October 25, 1879.)

Chief Ouray, the arrow, leader of the southern Utes. Indoctrination by the federal Indian Bureau which made him responsible for the actions of the various tribes was not acceptable to all. For his services, Ouray received an annual salary of $1,000 and a small house at Los Pinos Agency. (*Harper's Weekly*, October 25, 1879.)

The farm of Chief Ouray. (*Leslie's*, December 6, 1879.)

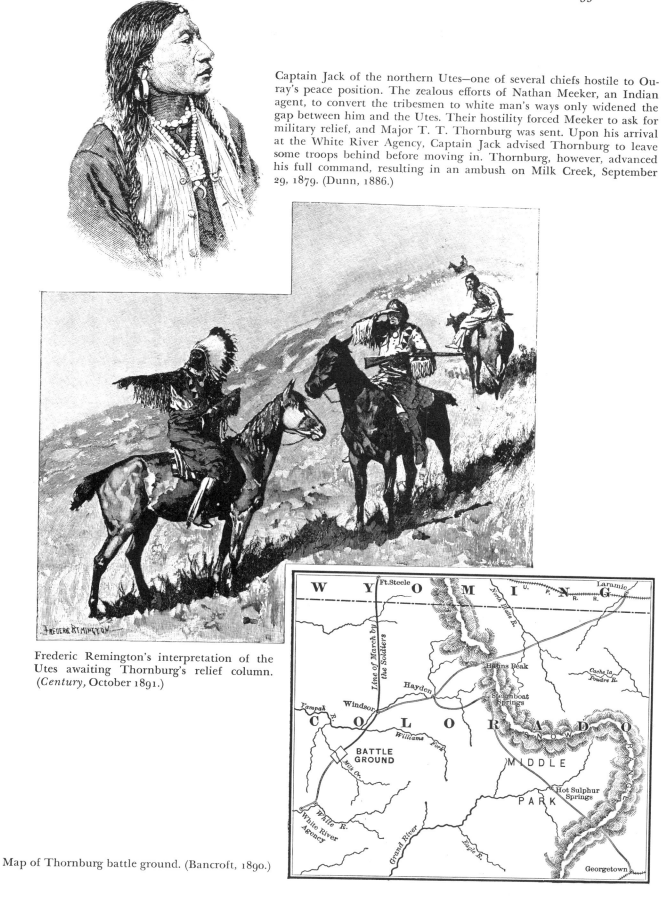

Captain Jack of the northern Utes—one of several chiefs hostile to Ouray's peace position. The zealous efforts of Nathan Meeker, an Indian agent, to convert the tribesmen to white man's ways only widened the gap between him and the Utes. Their hostility forced Meeker to ask for military relief, and Major T. T. Thornburg was sent. Upon his arrival at the White River Agency, Captain Jack advised Thornburg to leave some troops behind before moving in. Thornburg, however, advanced his full command, resulting in an ambush on Milk Creek, September 29, 1879. (Dunn, 1886.)

Frederic Remington's interpretation of the Utes awaiting Thornburg's relief column. (*Century,* October 1891.)

Map of Thornburg battle ground. (Bancroft, 1890.)

Thornburg's Last Charge—a highly imaginative sketch by H. Vielé. (*Harper's Weekly*, November 1, 1879.)

Douglas, chief of the White River Utes, hostile to the white man. (*Leslie's,* November 15, 1879.)

A Ute necklace and box for percussion caps. (*Leslie's,* November 15, 1879.)

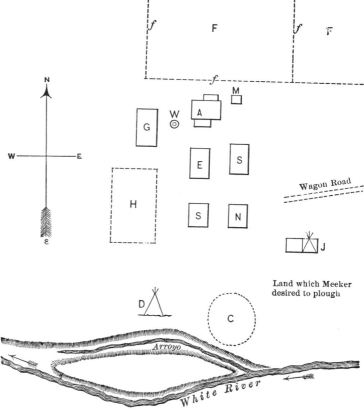

A. Agent's house.	G. Granary.
C. Corral.	H. Hay corral.
D. Douglas's teepee.	J. Johnson's house and lodge.
E. Employé's quarters.	M. Milk-house.
FF. Ploughed fields.	N. New building.
SS. Stores.	W. Well.

fff. Fences of enclosed fields.

Plan of the White River Agency as described by Chief Douglas. (Dunn, 1886.)

The attack on the White River Agency resulted in the deaths of twelve men, among them Meeker. Three women and two children were taken captive, and most of the buildings burned. This scene, sketched by C. A. H. McCauley, Third U.S. Cavalry, depicts the havoc resulting from the Indians' ferocity. (*Frank Leslie's Illustrated Newspaper*, December 6, 1879.)

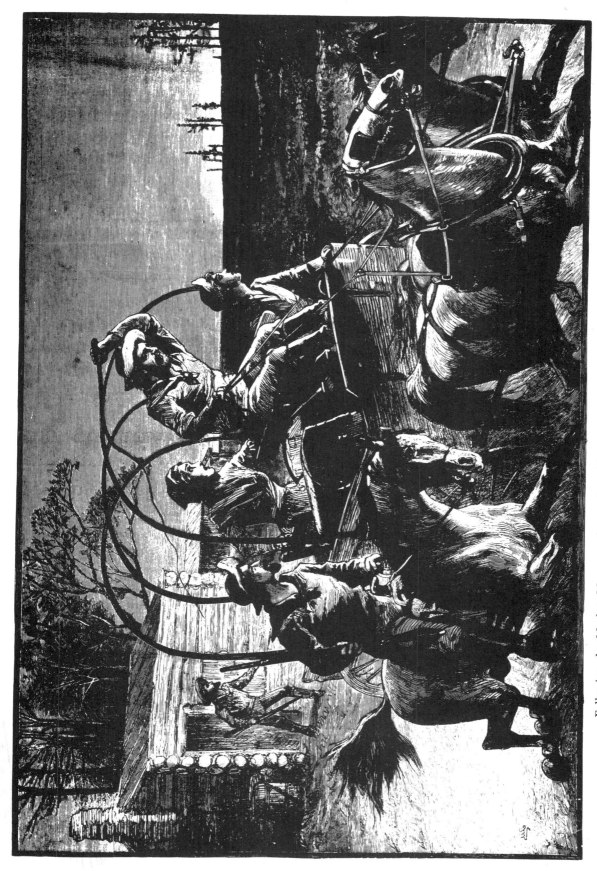

Following the Meeker Massacre, the northern Utes were moved from the White River area, but in 1877, Chief Colorow with a band of warriors attempted to reclaim the old hunting grounds. The terrified settlers, fearing an Indian uprising, fled. (*Leslie's*, September 3, 1887.)

In pursuit of Colorow. (*Harper's Weekly*, September 3, 1887.) Chief Colorow. (*Harper's Weekly*, October 25, 1879.) Troops and cattlemen engaged in a short, savage fight. Many Indians were slain and their horses captured; then, under military escort, the remaining insurgents returned to their reservation in Utah, thus ending Colorado's last Indian war.

"The Course of Empire"—a panorama of transportation—the old makes way for the new as man and beast move across the frontier. (*Harper's,* June 1867.)

Mired in gumbo, a not uncommon experience for the pioneers crossing the plains in early spring. (*Illustrated London News,* April 16, 1887.)

Round a campfire of buffalo chips on the plains at sunset, men drink coffee with guns in readiness and their stagecoach and guard nearby. (*Harper's,* July 1867.)

Postrider on winter delivery. (Crofutt, 1881.)

Prairie post office. (*Harper's* January 1880.)

END OF ISOLATION

LETTERS FROM DISTANT LOVED ONES were most welcome and read immediately. They arrived, both in fair and foul weather, by Pony Express, stagecoach, and lone postman on horseback.

"Lincoln Elected." The big news came to Julesburg by Pony Express and was relayed in the *Rocky Mountain News* to Colorado towns and mining camps. (Clampitt, 1889.)

Stagecoach-changing station, with fresh teams in readiness. (*Illustrated London News,* April 16, 1887.)

Weary stagecoach travelers gave their spirits a lift with a nip from the "friendly bottle." (*Leslie's,* May 28, 1881.)

The Leavenworth and Pikes Peak Express, the first passenger and mail service to reach Denver, arrived on May 7, 1859, with news from the Missouri river towns that was only one week old. (Ludlow, 1870.)

In the early days skis were referred to as "snow skates" and "snow shoes"—they bore no resemblance to the webbed snowshoes (shown). They were often used for transportation in the wilderness, especially by postmen who delivered mail to isolated communities.

Crossing the Rocky Mountains on "snow skates," an early reporter's term for skis. (Crofutt, 1881.)

A mountain postman on snowshoes. (*Illustrated London News,* October 30, 1880.)

During the first years of the gold rush a variety of supplies—food, whiskey, clothing, lumber, arms and ammunition, and equipment—was packed into the mining camps on horses and mules. (Crofutt, 1881.)

The bullwhacker and mule skinner—a rare breed of men—colorful in garb, weak in mind, and lusty in lingo. (*Illustrated London News,* April 16, 1887.)

"Ship" in "dock" on the plains. (Fossett, 1876.)

The bull train, drawn by six-to-twelve yoke of oxen and loaded with three-to-five tons of freight, had something for everybody. One such train took a load of cats to Denver and sold them at a good profit to miners who needed companionship and mousers. The bull train, like the steamboat, gave way to the railroad. (*Illustrated London News,* April 16, 1887.)

As the gold seekers pushed into the high country, transportation became more difficult. Enterprising men took advantage of the situation, constructed roads, and exacted tolls to pass over them. Otto Mears, the "Pathfinder of the San Juan," developed a 300-mile road system in the San Luis Valley.

Climbing into the high country on foot, on horseback, and by wagon. (Richardson, 1867.)

Toll gate—with a violation sign posted. (*Harper's Weekly*, September 3, 1881.)

$10 FINE FOR PASSING WITHOUT PAYING

The travois served the nomadic Indians well in moving their families and meager possessions from camp to camp. (Ludlow, 1870.)

Coast-to-coast telegraph lines across the plains brought direct communication to many isolated communities. (Clampitt, 1889.)

RUSH TO
THE ROCKIES

OVERNIGHT THE RUMOR OF GOLD in the Pikes Peak region changed many a man's life. In February of 1859, a wave of humanity surged westward to the land made magic by the word "Gold." On they came —the lucky ones in wagons or on horseback, the less fortunate pulling handcarts, pushing wheelbarrows, and on foot with a few possessions strapped to their backs. The cautious took the Overland and Santa Fe trails, the daring blazed a direct route—the Smoky Hill Trail.

Nothing thwarts the wheelbarrow emigrant. (*Leslie's*, April 30, 1859.)

In the spring of 1859, when the placers were exhausted, John H. Gregory discovered a rich lode on the North Fork of Clear Creek and saved the gold rush from total collapse. (Richardson, 1867.)

One man's daydream—to find gold by accident. (Thayer, 1887.)

By 1860 Denver was a typical frontier town with tents, log cabins, and several business blocks with two-story structures. In the bottomlands of the Platte an Arapahoe village added color to the rather drab community. (Richardson, 1867.)

The handcart emigrant did it the hard way. (*Leslie's,* April 30, 1859.)

Optimistic prospectors scour gulch and gully to pick and scratch for pay dirt. (*Illustrated London News*, April 17, 1880.)

The Pikes Peak gold rush was the first step of the filling-in process of the vast lands between the Missouri River and the settlements in California and Oregon.

A race to new diggings followed every report of a strike. (Ingersoll, 1883.)

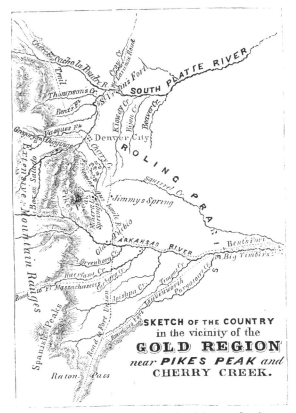

Map from an 1859 guidebook. (Marcy, 1859.)

Placer and vein mining required water to wash the "dirt." Sluices and flumes were built along the rocky walls of gulches to the base of operations. (Ingersoll, 1883.)

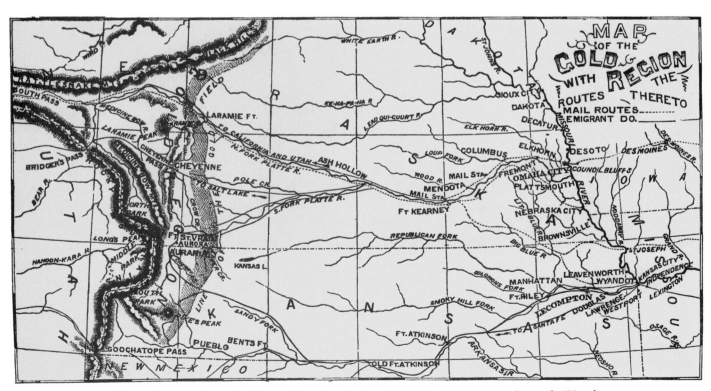

Maps of routes from the Missouri frontier to the gold fields were in great demand. (*Hand Book to the Gold Fields of Nebraska and Kansas*, 1859.)

To speed up the washing operation, the rocker or cradle, long tom, and sluices were devised, the latter especially in gulch mining. (Ingersoll, 1883.)

Some virgin deposits were so rich that gold could be dug with a knife or uncovered with a pick, then "washed" with a shovel and a pan. (Thayer, 1887.)

A mining camp extending through a gulch that was cluttered with buildings, mills, shaft houses, equipment, waste dumps, and sluices. (Smart, 1879.)

As placer mining became less profitable, it was replaced by hydraulic mining in a few places such as Lincoln City, at the head of French Gulch. In general, however, the country proved to be unsuitable for hydraulic mining. (Fossett, 1879.)

California Gulch, at an altitude of 10,000 feet, was discovered in April 1860 and became a mecca for thousands. Ora City stretched five miles along the gulch. (Mathews, 1866.)

A honeycombed mountain side. Drawn by the talented team of Paul Frenzeny and Jules Tavernier on their western trip in 1873. (*Harper's Weekly*, July 18, 1874.)

HIGH-COUNTRY ELDORADO

THE PLACER METHOD did not solve the problem of gold-bearing rock which had to be crushed to recover the metal. A simple, cheap, but tedious method for small-scale production was the Spanish arrastra, powered by draft animals or water. The ore was first reduced to a pulp and subjected to mercury to form an amalgam which united with the gold; finally, the elements were separated by heat.

Primitive horse-powered arrastra. (Richardson, 1867.)

Water-powered arrastra on Clear Creek. (Mathews, 1866.)

Double-handed drilling by two-man team. One man wields the blow while the other holds and turns the drill. (Fossett, 1879.)

Inspection after the shot. (*Illustrated London News,* April 7, 1877.)

Mine operators built stamp mills to overcome the difficulties of refractory ores. (Fossett, 1879.)

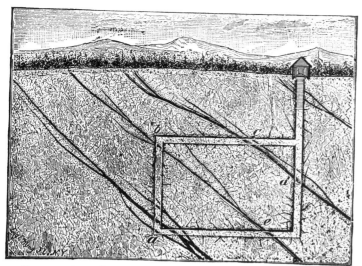

Cross section of a mine, showing veins, shaft, cross cuts, and winze. (Fossett, 1879.)

Cornish boys, miners from Cornwall, England, driving a tunnel. (*Illustrated London News,* April 7, 1877.)

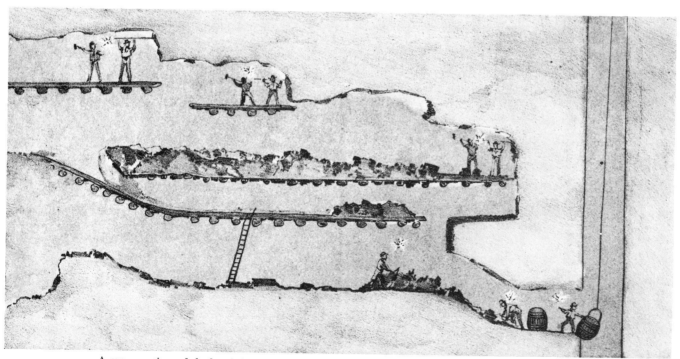

A cross section of shaft mining. The interior of No. 1 on the Gregory, owned by the Black Hawk Company. (Mathews, 1866.)

"SMELTING ORE IN COLORADO," a series of illustrations in *Harper's Weekly* by Frenzeny and Tavernier. Ore from the mines was subjected to crushing, calcining, washing, and smelting before being cast into bullion.

Crushing the ore. (*Harper's Weekly*, May 30, 1874.)

"Roasting" the gold and silver ore. (*Harper's Weekly*, May 30, 1874.)

Vats for leaching "roasted" ore. (Fossett, 1879.)

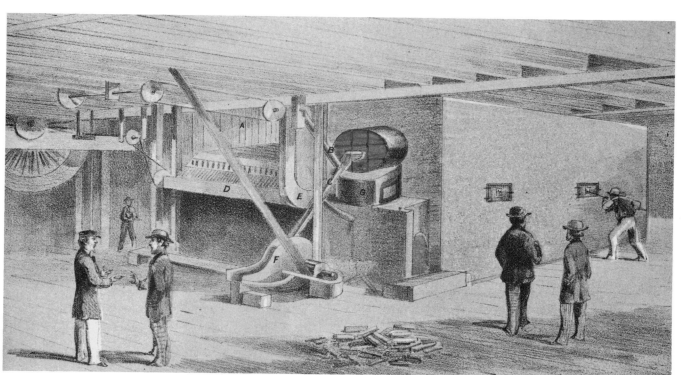

A lithograph showing how the furnace of the Keith process of the Hope Gold Company operates. (Mathews, 1866.)

Mine locomotive. (Thayer, 1887.)

Rock-boring winch.
(Thayer, 1887.)

Ingersoll rock drill and compressor
as advertised in 1881 by C. E.
Kennedy of Denver. (*State Business
Directory of Colorado,* 1881.)

The Bruckner cylinder for ore
reduction. (Fossett, 1876.)

Casting silver bricks. (*Harper's Weekly*, May 30, 1874.)

Removing bullion from the molds. (Miles, 1896.)

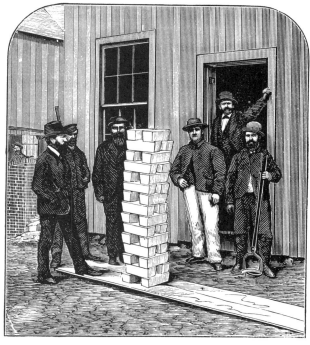

"Bullion shipment—a ton and a quarter of silver— value $45,000." (Fossett, 1876.)

Larimer Street, Denver, 1859. (Richardson, 1867.)

Bird's-eye view of Denver in 1859, a settlement of tents, log cabins, and Indian tepees. (Richardson, 1867.)

DENVER— QUEEN OF THE ROCKIES

IN APRIL 1860, the legislative assembly of Jefferson Territory moved to consolidate the Cherry Creek settlements, Auraria, the undeveloped St. Charles site, and Denver into one municipality. Two years later, the first territorial assembly of Colorado Territory approved this act. Of the two names, Denver and Auraria, Denver was the one accepted.

Early Denver. The building with tower (right) is the original mint, sketched by James F. Gookins. (*Harper's Weekly*, October 13, 1866.)

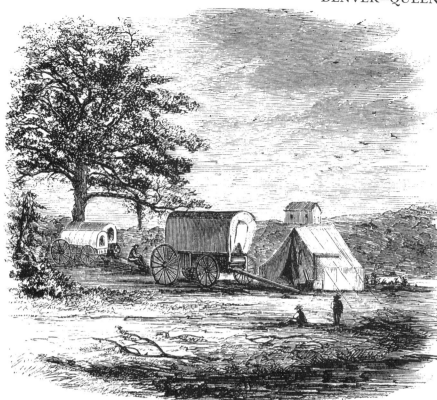

A prospective citizen camps on Cherry Creek. (*Leslie's*, August 20, 1859.)

The *New York Illustrated News,* October 4, 1862, erroneously featured this drawing of Auraria as the scene of a "horrible Indian massacre." A roving correspondent located the town in Minnesota and associated it with Sioux attacks. There were no serious Indian problems in Colorado at this time. (*New York Illustrated News,* October 4, 1862.)

In 1860, the Pikes Peak gold fields were legally in Arapahoe County, Kansas Territory. The above sketch by Colonel D. H. Huyett shows Auraria (left) on the west side of Cherry Creek with Longs Peak in the distance. The promoters of Denver City (right) "jumped the St. Charles lands." (*Leslie's*, December 15, 1860.)

Rocky Mountain News office. (Richardson, 1867.)

William N. Byers, founder and editor of the *Rocky Mountain News* (1859), the first newspaper in the Cherry Creek settlements. (Baskin, 1880.)

G. H. Hayes's sketch of the *News* staff, ready to defend the establishment against criminals enraged by newspaper criticism. (Richardson, 1867.)

Office of the Leavenworth and Pikes Peak Express Company, Denver City, Kansas Territory. The first stagecoach reached Denver June 7, 1859. (*Leslie's,* August 20, 1859.)

Theodore R. Davis's sketch of the Butterfield's Overland Dispatch office, which shared the building with C. A. Cook & Co. banking house (c. 1865). (*Harper's Weekly*, January 27, 1866.)

Miners bringing in gold dust to the C. A. Cook & Co. banking house. Butterfield's Overland Dispatch office opened in September 1865 with the arrival of the first coach. (*Harper's Weekly*, January 27, 1866.)

Major William Gilpin was appointed by President Lincoln as governor of the Colorado Territory (1861-62). (Baskin, 1880.)

Dr. John Evans, second governor of the territory (1862-65), served his adopted state well during the troublesome years of the Civil War. (Baskin, 1880.)

Residence of Governor John Evans, 14th and Arapahoe streets. A historical building destroyed, unfortunately, as Denver grew. (Baskin, 1880.)

Looking northeast on Larimer Street, Denver.
(Fossett, 1879.)

Miners wait for mail at the Central Overland
California & Pikes Peak Express Company.
(Richardson, 1867.)

View of Denver identified as showing the Cherry Creek flood of 1864. (*Le Tour du Monde,*
1868.)

For the "swingers" of that day, Denver's Hells Acre offered every variety of amusement. T. R. Davis's sketch, "A Gambling Scene in Denver City," is characteristic of frontier towns throughout the West. (*Harper's Weekly*, February 17, 1866.)

The old U.S. Mint, Denver.
(Wood, 1889.)

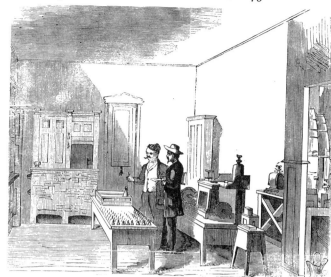

Assay Room—U.S. Mint, Colorado Territory. (*Harper's Weekly,* October 13, 1866.)

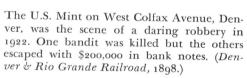

The U.S. Mint on West Colfax Avenue, Denver, was the scene of a daring robbery in 1922. One bandit was killed but the others escaped with $200,000 in bank notes. (*Denver & Rio Grande Railroad,* 1898.)

Union Bank of Denver, corner of Arapahoe and 16th Streets. Insert shows the burglar-proof safe. (O'Ryan and Malone, 1889.)

U.S. Court House and Post Office, Denver. (Wood, 1889.)

A SHIELD with three white peaks in chief,
  A pick and sledge beneath them crossed;
For crest, an eye with rays; a sheaf
  Of reeds about an ax; and tossed
About its base a scroll I see,
That says, "*Nil sine numine.*"

The State Seal, probably designed by Lewis L. Weld, first secretary of the Colorado Territory. (Baskin, 1881.)

The State Capitol constructed of gray granite from the Gunnison area. Crowned by a dome embellished with "Colorado's Glory"—250 ounces of gold leaf, it dominated Denver until recent high-rise structures appeared. (*Harper's*, May 1888.)

Court House, City and County of Denver, 16th Street between Court Place and Tremont Street, demolished in 1934. (Wood, 1889.)

Old City Hall at 14th and Larimer streets was the scene of the "City Hall War," March 15, 1894. (*Harper's*, May 1888.)

The St. James, representative of the affluent times. (*Rocky Mountain Official Railway Guide,* 1894.)

THE GROWTH OF DENVER in the era of the great silver camps was phenomenal. Between 1880 and 1890 the population increased from 35,629 to 106,713. The wealth from this mining boom resulted in an expansion of building and business. The small inns, taverns, and hotels could no longer accommodate the swelling population and influx of visitors. Grand hotels of brick and stone were built and attracted the free-spending gold, silver, cattle, and railroad "kings."

Hotel Victor, 18th and Larimer streets, built before the boom. (*Rocky Mountain Official Railway Guide,* November 1897.)

The Albany, 17th and Stout streets. Recently, after much publicity, it was saved from the axe and renovated.

The Windsor, built in 1880 at 1815 Larimer Street with the aid of English money, was modeled after a Montreal hotel of the same name. For years it was the center of numerous social activities. Here the impoverished H. A. W. Tabor, former Silver King of Leadville, died in 1899. (Baskin, 1880.)

Brown Palace Hotel, 17th Street and Tremont Place, built of red Arizona stone by pioneer H. C. Brown. Many Denverites and visitors still consider it *the* hotel. Much festivity prevails here, particularly during the annual National Western Stock Show and Rodeo when everything and everybody—from prize bulls to cowboys—are in evidence. (*Denver Real Estate and Stock Exchange,* 1891-92.)

Hotel Metropole and Broadway Theater—the latter a rival of the Tabor Grand in the 1890s. (*Denver Real Estate and Stock Exchange*, 1891-92.)

Olympic Theater, 1737-39 Market Street. (*Souvenir des Denver Turnvereins*, 1890.)

Ornate East Indian interior of the Broadway Theater. (*Denver Real Estate and Stock Exchange*, 1891-92.)

Old Turner Hall, Market Street, later the Central Theater. In 1885, Laura Le Claire, a burlesque queen, held forth in "wild abandon." (*Souvenir des Denver Turnvereins*, 1890.)

H. A. W. Tabor, fabulous Silver King of Leadville. This uncouth, warm-hearted, generous storekeeper, whose touch turned everything into silver, died destitute at the end of the century. (*Harper's*, May 1888.)

Tabor Grand Opera House opened in 1881. It attracted the fashionable set—mining and cattle kings, smelter magnates, merchant princes, and distinguished thespians from abroad. (*Harper's*, May 1888.)

The National Mining and Industrial Exposition, 1882. A showcase for ores, geological specimens, and mining machinery exhibited by U.S. and foreign manufacturers. (*Harper's Weekly*, May 27, 1882.)

"Red Light District," Denver. (Western Collection, Denver Public Library.)

WHETHER THE SHADY LADIES were called fallen angels or skidoo babes, soiled doves or harlots, respectable women protested these "Jezebels beyond redemption." The pleasure houses along Holladay Street became so brazen that out of respect for the pioneer stageline owner, Ben Holladay, for whom the street had been named, the name was changed to the equally apt Market Street. The names of Mattie Silks, Blanche Brown, Jennie Rogers, and Ella Wellington are written forever into the lusty history of Denver.

Saturday Night in a Denver bagnio. (Western Collection, Denver Public Library.)

IN 1864, the Methodist Episcopal Church established Colorado Seminary. Sixteen years later it became the University of Denver, a degree-granting institution.

Colorado Seminary. (Richardson, 1867.)

University of Denver—for both sexes. (Crofutt, 1881.)

Westminster University, originally a Presbyterian Church college, later a theological school for the Pillar of Fire Church. (*Denver Real Estate and Stock Exchange,* 1891-92.)

Wolfe Hall, an Episcopal finishing school for girls, opened in 1868. (Baskin, 1880.)

Governor Frederick W. Pitkin faced labor and Indian problems during his two-term administration, 1879-83. (Baskin, 1880.)

A view of the city in the early 1880s from an unidentified church steeple. (Riding, 1882.)

Chamber of Commerce. (*Union Pacific Sketch Book,* 1887.)

View of 14th Street, a tree-lined, dirt road looking west to the heart of the city. (Wood, 1889.)

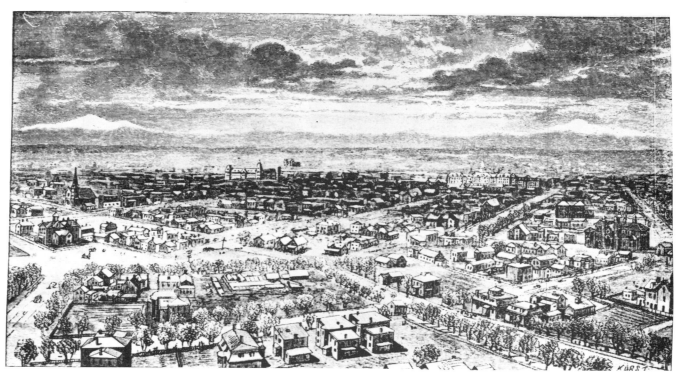

Bird's-eye view of Denver in the late 1880s. (Beaugrand, 1890.)

Methodist Episcopal Church, affectionately called the "Old Lawrence Street Church," stood on the southwest corner of 14th and Lawrence streets. (Richardson, 1867.)

St. John's Episcopal Cathedral, 20th and Welton streets, destroyed by fire in 1903. (*Harper's*, May 1888.)

Central Presbyterian Church, 18th and Champa streets. Some views show it without the spire. (Baskin, 1880.)

Father Joseph R. Machebeuf, sent to the "Pikes Peak Region" by Bishop J. B. Lamy, Santa Fe Diocese, arrived in Denver on October 29, 1860. Named first bishop of Denver in 1868, Machebeuf was a man of energy and devotion who rightly deserved the epithet, "apostle of Catholicism in Colorado." (Baskin, 1880.)

Proposed Cathedral of the Immaculate Conception, East Colfax Avenue and Logan Street. The twin-spired Indiana-limestone building in French-Gothic design was not completed until 1912. (*Denver Republican,* March 18, 1888.)

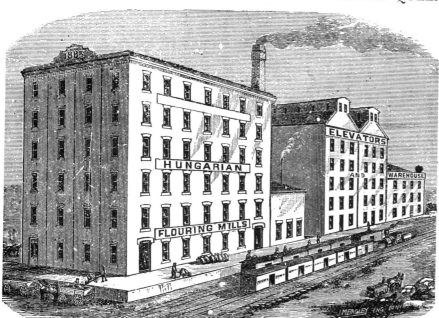

Hungarian Flour Mills, built in 1883, on Wazee, between 7th and 8th streets. (O'Ryan and Malone, 1889.)

Nathaniel P. Hill, metallurgist from Brown University, solved the major problems of Colorado's refractory ores. He organized the Boston and Colorado Smelter Company and in 1868 erected in Blackhawk the first smelter in the Colorado Territory. (*Harper's*, May 1888.)

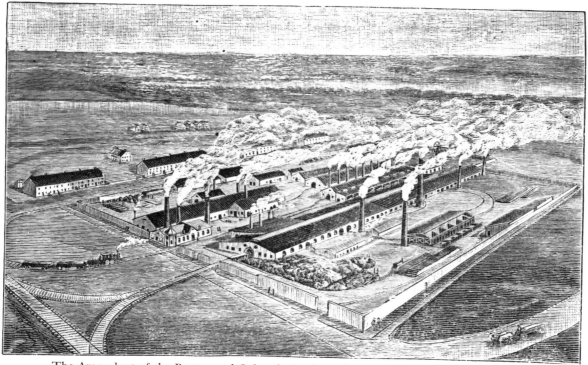

The Argo plant of the Boston and Colorado Smelting Company. (*Denver Real Estate and Stock Exchange*, 1891-92.)

CLEAR CREEK— MINERAL EMPIRE

IN THE EARLY STAGES of the gold rush there was little distinction between placer and vein (or lode) mining. Some claims were true placer deposits; others were heavily eroded, crumbled outcroppings of veins near the surface.

Even before the fabulous 1859 ended, gold lured miners and adventurers southward to South Park, then to the west across the Continental Divide into the valleys of the rivers draining toward the Pacific Ocean. Shortly thereafter gold seekers pushed southward to the remote San Juan country.

By 1860 it was clear that Colorado's mineral wealth lay in a broad belt stretching diagonally across the territory from the San Juan region to Boulder County in the northeast, a direct-line distance of some 200 miles.

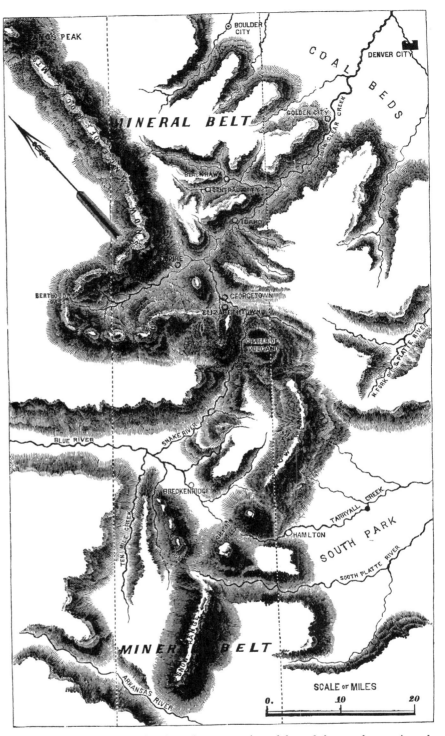

Map of the first penetration into the mountain gulches of the northern mineral belt. (*Harper's,* June 1867.)

For several years Golden, founded in 1859, rivaled Denver as political capital (1862-67) and supply center. (Fossett, 1876.)

By the 1880s Golden was an active manufacturing center—flour mills, two breweries, a paper mill, and three brick kilns. (Denver and Rio Grande Railroad, 1878.)

Jarvis Hall, founded in Golden in 1869, by Rt. Reverend G. M. Randall, missionary Episcopal bishop, to train young men in technical mining. An 1870 legislative appropriation resulted in further development, and in 1874 Jarvis Hall became the Colorado School of Mines. (Baskin, 1880.)

The
Golden
Brewery.
(Baskin, 1880.)

Smelting Works (left to right): Golden Smelting, Malachite, French Smelting, and Moore
Mining and Smelting. (Baskin, 1880.)

From Golden to the mountain camps of Idaho City, Mill City, and Empire City the Colorado Central Rail-road climbed up Clear Creek Canyon. (*Illustrated London News,* August 15, 1885.)

Idaho Springs—first known as Jackson's Diggings, then Sacramento City, and finally Idaho City—was founded January 1859 at the mouth of Chicago Creek. George A. Jackson's discovery, the richest placer at that time, and John H. Gregory's find assured the region's golden future. (Mathews, 1866.)

THE GOLDEN DREAMS of fortune hunters were fulfilled in Black Hawk, Nevadaville, and Central City. In 1861, when Colorado Territory was established, Gilpin County with Central City as the county seat became the "little kingdom of Gilpin" and was the mainstay of the struggling territory.

Black Hawk—a mining camp with mills, smelters, business houses, and a church. (*Harper's,* June 1867.)

Nevadaville with Bald Mountain in the background. (Fossett, 1876.)

Central City, midway up the gulch, is considered the oldest of Colorado's surviving mountain towns. (*Harper's*, June 1867.)

Eureka Street, Central City, still retains much of its original flavor. In 1873, silver bricks made a pathway on which President U.S. Grant walked from the stagecoach to the Teller House. (Fossett, 1876.)

Henry M. Teller, prominent pioneer of Gregory Gulch. He and Jerome B. Chaffee were the first U.S. senators from Colorado. (*Harper's*, May 1888.)

Empire, the last of the mining towns on the road to Berthoud Pass. (*Harper's*, June 1867.)

The Barton House, the first pretentious hotel in Georgetown, built in 1867. (Georgetown Courier, 1886.)

The Georgetown Loop, the fabulous narrow-gauge tracks of the Colorado and Southern Railroad, was one of the most spectacular scenic rides in the West. (*Rocky Mountain Official Railway Guide*, 1897.)

Berthoud Pass, 11,315 feet elevation. (Georgetown Courier, 1886.)

Silver Plume, 1870, and the Dives-Pelican Mines. (Fossett, 1879.)

Georgetown, at the foot of the Continental Divide, sprang up with a gold discovery in 1859. By 1939, its total production of silver, gold, copper, lead, and zinc, was estimated at some $90 million. (Fossett, 1876.)

The Pay-Rock Mine and tramway at Georgetown. (Georgetown Courier, 1886.)

The Comstock, owned by the Boston Silver Mining Company, leading mine at Montezuma (1869). (Greatorex, 1873.)

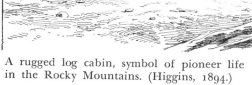

A rugged log cabin, symbol of pioneer life in the Rocky Mountains. (Higgins, 1894.)

The expansion of the mining frontier in Colorado was important because it brought the first large settlement groups to the mountain regions.

Grays Peak, named in honor of botanist Asa Gray, towers 14,270 feet above an Indian camp. (Tenney, 1880.)

W. A. Rogers captured the lively enthusiasm with which the first stagecoach was greeted in a mountain camp. (*Harper's Weekly*, November 10, 1883.)

Kokomo, Ten Mile Mining District, was founded "upon vast expectations." Prospectors still have faith in the region. (*Harper's*, March 1880.)

A hair-raising ride when the drivers lived up to their boasts. (*Harper's*, February 1880.)

BOULDER

In October 1858, Captain Thomas Aikens led a small party to the mouth of Boulder Canyon. The town of Boulder became the gateway to the rich gold run in the Gold Hill area and was the commerical center for the mountain camps.

Boulder Creek with the celebrated Flatirons in the background, three majestic bulwarks of red rock strata, a challenge to experienced and novice climbers alike. (Ferris, 1886.)

Following the lean 1860s, Boulder City was incorporated in 1871 and with the coming of two railroads and the founding of the University of Colorado (1876) looked forward to a promising future. (Fossett, 1876.)

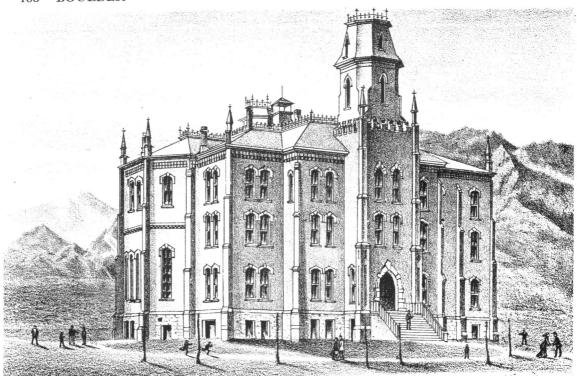

The University of Colorado, created by legislative action and the support of Boulder's public-spirited citizens who donated both land and money, opened in 1877 in one building—Old Main. (Baskin, 1880.)

The first public school in Colorado was erected in Boulder in 1860 at 15th and Walnut streets. Central School, on the same site, is still in use as a school service center. (Baskin, 1880.)

First Boulder County Courthouse, erected 1860. (Hall, 1891.)

Boulder Colorado Sanitarium, now Boulder Memorial Hospital, at the mouth of Sunshine Canyon on West Mapleton Avenue, opened in 1898 under the auspices of the Seventh-Day Adventist denomination. (Denver & Rio Grande Railroad, 1898.)

Central School, on the same site as the original (shown), is still in use as a school service center. (Baskin, 1880.)

Boulder Creek still lures seekers of another kind of gold—the beauty of the mountain. (Ingham, 1880.)

Boulder Falls in Boulder Canyon, the gift of Charles G. Buckingham to the City in 1914. (Kansas Pacific Railroad, 1875.)

North Boulder silver mill. (Fossett, 1876.)

Caribou, a silver camp, boomed to a town of 3,000 in the 1870s. (Tice, 1872.)

Caribou silver mill at Nederland, an important milling and shipping center for ores in the vicinity. (Fossett, 1876.)

Gold is still found along South Boulder Creek near Rollinsville. (Baskin, 1880.)

GATEWAY TO THE GODS

In 1858, the Lawrence Party of Pikes Peakers camped on the site of the future Colorado City (later Colorado Springs). A year later, when the gold seekers swarmed in, efforts to establish law and order resulted in the El Paso Claims Club. (Richardson, 1867.)

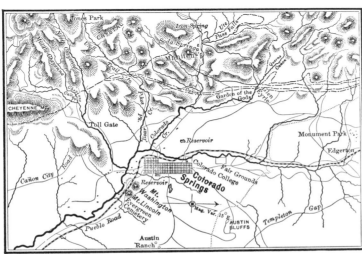

Map of Colorado Springs and vicinity. (Bancroft, 1890.)

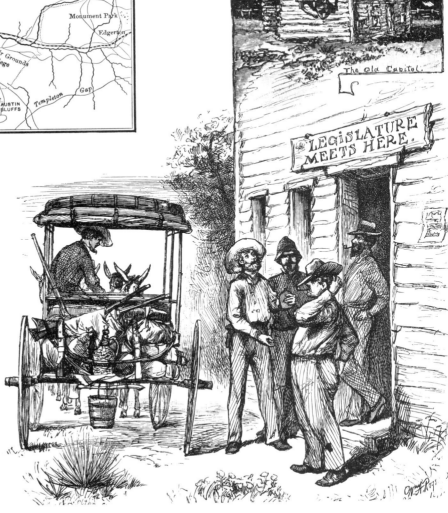

Colorado Territory had several capitals. In 1862, Colorado City (now Colorado Springs), had a four-day spell of being the capital, then the title shifted to Golden. State officials, however, transacted their business in Denver. (Hayes, 1880.)

Earlier titles of Fountain Creek—*Fontaine qui Bouille, Rio del Sacramento,* and *Rio del Almagre*—illustrate the French and Spanish influence in the territory. (Richardson, 1867.)

W. A. Rogers's interpretation of relaxation at the El Paso Club. (*Harper's,* January 1880.)

In the state census of 1885 the English constituted one-fourth of the foreign population. ". . . as the English, despite their idiosyncracies are an enjoyment-loving people, they never fail to enjoy themselves, whether sunned at the tropics or chilled at the poles."

Colorado Springs (c. 1880s) with snow-capped Pikes Peak in the distance was often referred to as "Little Lunnon" because of the number of young Englishmen who settled there. (Jackson, 1878.)

The prosperity, resulting from mining, ranching, and farming, brought about marked changes in civic, cultural, and social advances. Most towns boasted handsome buildings—business blocks, churches, opera houses, hotels, and railroad stations—a proud display for visitors in the mountain state.

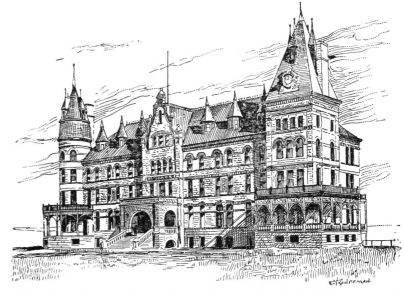

The Union Printers Home, initially financed by G. W. Childs and A. J. Drexel of the *Public Ledger,* Philadelphia, was erected in 1892 on 80 acres, the gift of the local board of trade. (Denver & Rio Grande Railroad, 1898.)

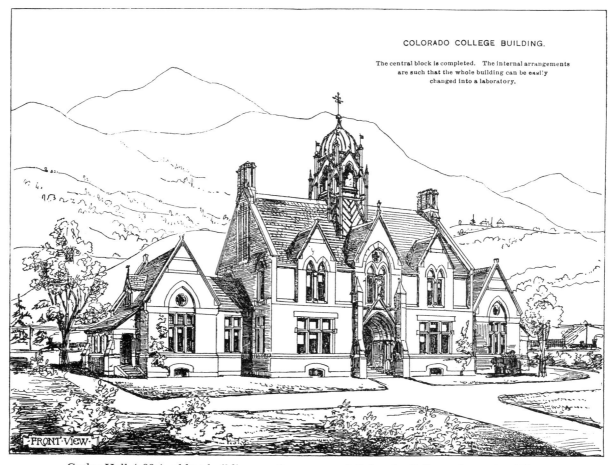

COLORADO COLLEGE BUILDING.

The central block is completed. The internal arrangements are such that the whole building can be easily changed into a laboratory.

FRONT·VIEW·

Cutler Hall (1880), oldest building on the campus of Colorado College. General William J. Palmer, prominent citizens, and the Congregational Church were the founders and benefactors. (Tenney, 1880.)

Curiously eroded stone formations in Monument Park, 20 miles north of Colorado Springs. Early visitors, who named the park, mentioned its eerie atmosphere and saw in the rocks many likenesses—from pagan temples to Spanish friars, from savage chiefs to knights in armor. (Tenney, 1880.)

"Natural Monuments," the lithographer's title for these strange outcroppings. (Mathews, 1868-69.)

The Antlers, 1882, a plush hotel in Colorado Springs, demolished recently to make way for a larger hotel and a business complex. (*Rocky Mountain Official Railway Guide*, 1896.)

Williams Canyon—a deep, rugged gash in the mountains—narrows until the walls project over the valley floor. (Baskin, 1881.)

Cheyenne Falls, known today as Seven Falls, near Colorado Springs. (Tenney, 1880.)

The natural gateway to the Garden of the Gods affords a view of Pikes Peak between Gray and Red Rocks. (Richardson, 1867.)

Ute Pass, a stronghold of the Indians until they gave way to the pressures of the fifty-niners. (Greatorex, 1873.)

One account says that R. E. Cable bestowed the name on this famous area when he first beheld it in 1859 with a Mr. Beach. The latter remarked, "This would be a fine place for a beergarden." "Beergarden?" questioned Cable. "Why this is a fit place for the gods to assemble—a garden of the gods!" he exclaimed. (*Scribner's, August* 1876.)

THE INDIANS regarded the great springs at Manitou as a place of safe retreat. French traders also visited here, and Frémont during his 1843 expedition analyzed the water.

Soda Springs and Cliff House at Manitou. (*Scribner's,* August 1876.)

Bathhouses and hotels at Manitou Springs with Pikes Peak in the background. (Baskin, 1881.)

Iron Springs Hotel, Manitou. (Buckman, 1892-93.)

Little Minnehaha Falls on the Pikes Peak Trail. (*Lippincott's*, January 1883.)

"On the road to Pikes Peak." (*Harper's Weekly*, July 23, 1887.)

Pikes Peak as seen from the Denver and Canyon Road. (Mathews, 1870.)

"We looked upon four territories of the Union—Kansas, Nebraska, Utah and New Mexico. . . ." Thus, Albert Richardson described the view from the summit of Pikes Peak. (Richardson, 1867.)

Predecessor of the Weather Bureau. A U.S. Signal Station on the summit of Pikes Peak, 1873, studied the combination of high altitude and accessibility. (Ingham, 1880.)

The engine of the Pikes Peak cogwheel railroad, built by the Baldwin Locomotive Works, traveled eight miles an hour. (Denver & Rio Grande Railroad, 1896.)

IT WAS AN ESTABLISHED FACT that gold existed in the Cripple Creek district, but no one believed that mining would be profitable. In January 1891, cowboy Robert Womack announced in Colorado Springs a new discovery. The following rush and new strikes created a fantastic boom and one of the richest gold camps in the U.S.—$15 million annually for a decade. In 1893 W. A. Rogers sketched scenes of the Cripple Creek boom.

"An outdoor smithy." (*Harper's Weekly,* December 23, 1893.)

"A street scene at night." (*Harper's Weekly,* December 23, 1893.)

"Mining camp architecture." (*Harper's Weekly,* December 23, 1893.)

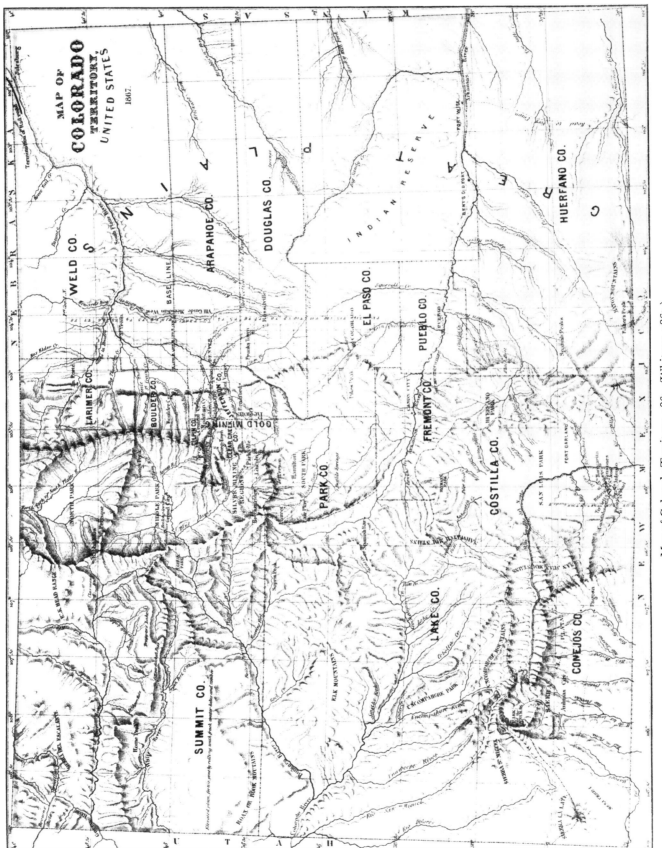

Map of Colorado Territory, 1867. (Whitney, 1867.)

WEBS
OF
STEEL

THE ROCKY MOUNTAINS created serious transportation problems, but Coloradoans were determined to bring the railroads through the Territory. When the first line, the Union Pacific, balked at the rocky barrier, the Denver Pacific, in 1870, connected the capital with the transcontinental road. Shortly thereafter, the Kansas Pacific Railroad lengthened the territory's trail of iron with connections eastward to St. Louis and Kansas City.

In 1871, General William J. Palmer established the Denver & Rio Grande which within a year reached Pueblo and continued along the Arkansas River to Florence. Palmer, after successive court suits with the Santa Fe Railway, finally won the battle over rights to the Royal Gorge via Marshall Pass. This scenic, breathtaking road is the highest transcontinental traverse in North America.

Over the Sangre de Cristo Mountains via the Denver & Rio Grande Railroad. (Fossett, 1879.)

Map, showing Colorado railroads. (Bancroft, 1890.)

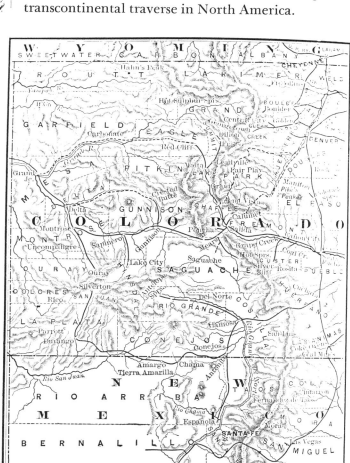

Water tank on the Atchison, Topeka & Santa Fe Railway. (Fossett, 1876.)

Construction train with tie and track men. (*Harper's*, June 1867.)

Approaching a station on the plains in semiarid, treeless, eastern Colorado. (*Illustrated London News*, August 15, 1885.)

"Denver Pacific U.S. Mail." (*Daily Colorado Tribune*, June 22, 1870.)

First Denver Railroad Station, Wazee Street: Kansas Pacific and Denver Pacific railroads (right), and probably the Colorado Central Railroad (left). Tramways are at far left of the station. (Western Collection, Colorado State Historical Society.)

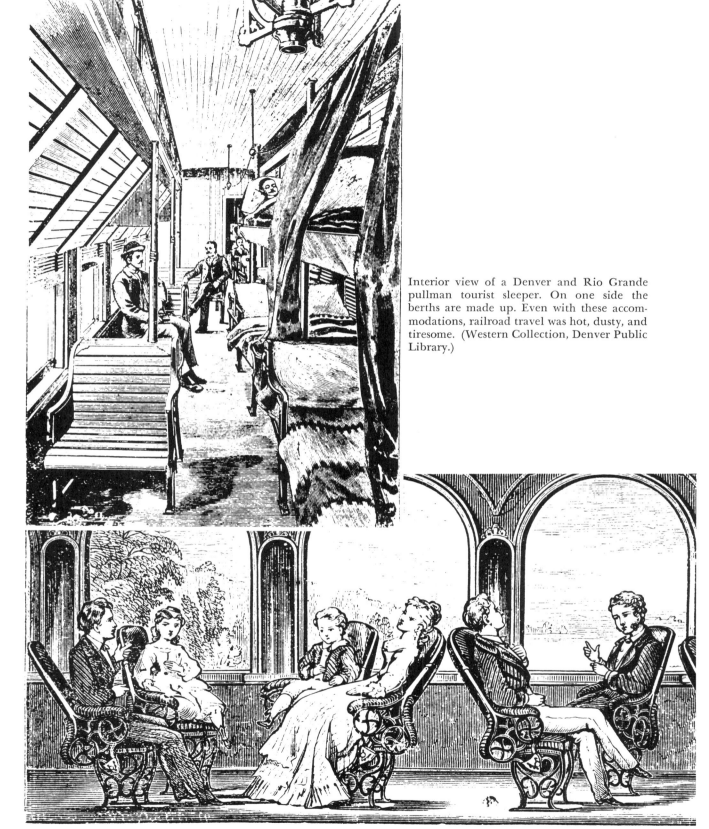

Interior view of a Denver and Rio Grande pullman tourist sleeper. On one side the berths are made up. Even with these accommodations, railroad travel was hot, dusty, and tiresome. (Western Collection, Denver Public Library.)

The reclining-seat car permitted the passengers to face in various directions for viewing outside and visiting inside. (*Official Guide of Chicago, Kansas City, and Denver Short Line, February* 1875.)

Scenery along the Denver & Rio Grande Railway through La Veta Pass. (Fossett, 1879.)

Colorado Central Railroad Station at Beaver Brook Junction. (Fossett, 1876.)

The Atchison, Topeka & Santa Fe's torturous route over Raton Pass (7,834 ft.) to New Mexico. (Fossett, 1879.)

The wind wagon, a "telegraph repair car," moved on the rails with the aid of wind sails to carry workers to the trouble sites. (*Harper's Weekly,* December 14, 1878.)

"Comet," one of the Union Pacific's crack trains, approaching Julesburg. Betting on antelope that sometimes raced the train along the tracks provided an exciting and amusing sport for the passengers. (Clampitt, 1889.)

LEADVILLE—SILVER CAMPS

"High Line" wagon road over Loveland Pass from the Georgetown terminal of the Colorado Central. Daily, in 1879, hundreds of wagons brought in supplies. (*Illustrated London News*, May 28, 1881.)

Leadville, a boom town of warehouses, lodgings, tents, hotels, churches, breweries, saloons, restaurants, theaters, and so forth, proudly called itself the "Magic City." (Fossett, 1879.)

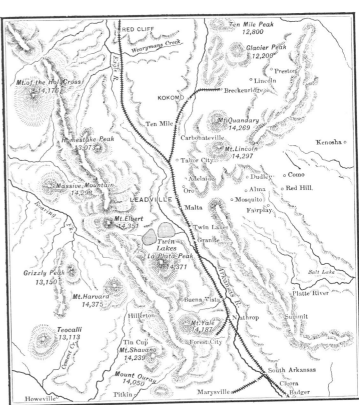

Map of Leadville and vicinity. (Bancroft, 1890.)

Freighting on Mosquito Pass (13,180 ft.). A hair-raising experience in the 1870s and still a spectacular ride for the venturous. (*Harper's,* February 1880.)

Twin Lakes (9,210 ft.), south of Leadville, the "Cloud City." (Tenney, 1880.)

At first glance Leadville was a disappointment, but with mines, smelters, and "night life" in saloons, it became Babylon. (*Harper's,* February 1880.)

Tenderfeet—in more ways than one. (*Illustrated London News,* May 28, 1881.)

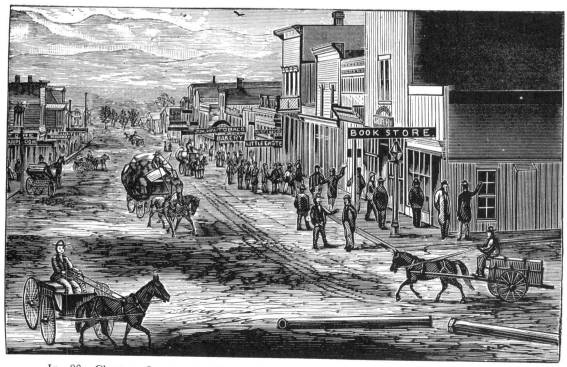

In 1880, Chestnut Street, one of Leadville's important thoroughfares, was paved with slag from the smelters. (Ingham, 1880.)

Accommodations in the new mining camp of Leadville were inadequate and expensive. E. Jump sketches miners and emigrants asleep on the sawdust floor of a billiard saloon—at "two-bits a night." (*Leslie's, Supplement,* June 7, 1879.)

The disappointment, poor food and sanitary conditions, starvation, and various illnesses—especially from venereal disease and pneumonia—claimed scores of the population in their struggle for wealth in the mining camps. To keep the rising death toll secret, burials took place at night in unmarked graves. (*Harper's,* February 1880.)

Any gathering was appropriate for "sluicing the inner man." (*Harper's Weekly, Supplement,* March 28, 1874.)

The raw town grew in all directions. Shacks, lean-tos, tents, and cabins sprang up overnight along stretches of sidewalks, none of which was on the same level. Nightly, the streets were the stage for riotous celebrants—men and women of all ages and professions. (*Scribner's,* October 1879.)

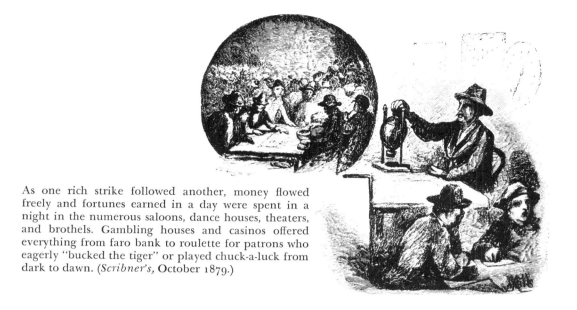

As one rich strike followed another, money flowed freely and fortunes earned in a day were spent in a night in the numerous saloons, dance houses, theaters, and brothels. Gambling houses and casinos offered everything from faro bank to roulette for patrons who eagerly "bucked the tiger" or played chuck-a-luck from dark to dawn. (*Scribner's,* October 1879.)

Everywhere in the "wonderful mining town of Leadville" humanity indulged in revelry of every kind. (*Leslie's,* July 12, 1879.)

Fryer Hill honored George Fryer who named the rich strike of carbonate ore "New Discovery." On this hill August Rische and George Hook, grubstaked by Horace Tabor, struck the lode yielding $8,000 a day. This "Little Pittsburgh" sparked the opening of new mines which stockpiled the fortunes of the "Silver Kings." (*Illustrated London News*, May 28, 1881.)

At the Leadville post office men stood in line for two hours at four delivery windows. (*Leslie's*, May 3, 1879.)

The cabins of presumptuous squatters on ore-bearing lands in the mining districts were swiftly demolished by the miners. (*Leslie's, May 3, 1879.*)

Exterior and interior of Schayer's whole-sale liquor establishment. (*Leadville, Lake County and the Gold Belt*, 1895.)

The home of William H. James on Capitol Hill, Leadville, illustrates the typical clapboard, gingerbread style of architecture. (Baskin, 1881.)

Hotel Vendome opened in 1885. Its modified mansard roof, ornate cupola, and iron roof-trim mark it as late Victorian. (*Colorado's Enterprising Cities,* 1893.)

Elaborate dining room of Hotel Vendome. (*Leadville, Lake County and Gold Belt,* 1895.)

Sand's Brothers, haberdashers. (*Leadville, Lake County and Gold Belt,* 1895.)

The bar of Hotel Vendome boasted the best stock of liquor in Colorado. (*Leadville, Lake County and Gold Belt,* 1895.)

In 1879, J. J. McRobbie, "Clothing and Gents' Furnishing Goods," was located at 600-602 Harrison Avenue. (*Colorado's Enterprising Cities,* 1893.)

American National Bank, a handsome building of stone and brick, established in 1889. (*Colorado's Enterprising Cities,* 1893.)

Leadville's Second Ward School Building. (Baskin, 1881.)

The Leonard Shaft of the Matchless Mine, one of the bonanzas in the Leadville district. Tabor, impoverished at the time of his death in 1899, admonished his wife Baby Doe to "hold on to the Matchless." She did and died penniless and abandoned in 1935. (Baskin, 1881.)

The main shaft of the Little Chief Mine, one of the foremost during the bonanza. (Baskin, 1881.)

For several years the Carbonate (shown), Morning Star, Chrysolite, Catalpa, Little Pitts-burgh, Matchless, Iron Silver, and other celebrated mines held production at around $10 million annually. (Baskin, 1881.)

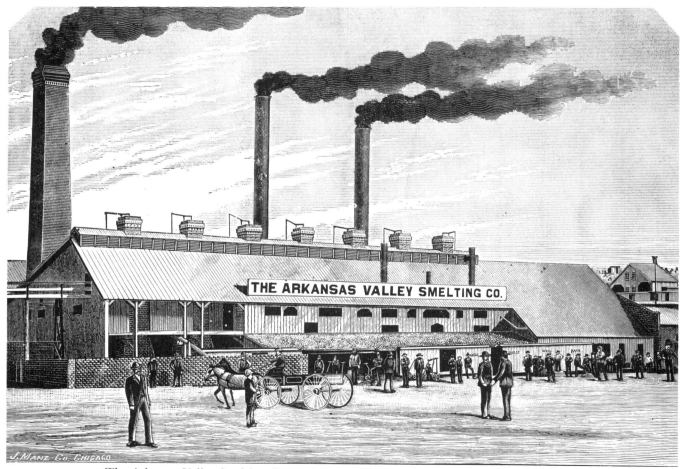

The Arkansas Valley Smelting Company, one of some two dozen in the Leadville region. (Union Pacific Railroad Company, 1887.)

Park City, near Leadville, may have been another name for Adelaide City. In this sketch the Sisters of Mercy, in their distinctive garb, collect funds for a new hospital. (*Leslie's,* April 12, 1879.)

"Fairplay," reputedly named by a group of prospectors expelled from Tarryall where settled miners guarded their finds. In the center of the town, the grave of Prunes, the famous burro, has an appropriate marker. (Greatorex, 1873.)

Mount of the Holy Cross (14,005 ft.), unknown before 1869. The sketches by Thomas Moran and the poem, "Cross of Snow," by Henry Wadsworth Longfellow attracted the world's attention to this sacred symbol. (Baskin, 1881.)

HEALTH AND RECREATION

COLORADO'S NATURAL GIFTS—wholesome climate, lofty mountains, quiet valleys, crystalline streams, and endless plains—invited the early settlers. Then there were the rumors of gold, but even before that, the great Colorado wilderness where buffalo, antelope, deer, and bear abounded was recognized as a hunter's paradise. And when word reached outside that Indians had long bathed their sick in Colorado's healing waters, a new type of emigrant, the health seeker, came in scores.

Idaho Springs, near Jackson's diggings, had elaborate accommodations for health seekers. (Crofutt, 1881.)

Glenwood Springs, originally Defiance, established in 1882, was developed as a health resort in 1891 by a British syndicate. (Sweetser, 1890.)

Pagosa Springs (Indian healing water) prospered as a health spa. The spring waters (average temperature of 153°) were used for many years to heat public buildings. (Fossett, 1879.)

In the late 1860s railroads sponsored excursions for buffalo hunting on the plains. (*London Illustrated News,* October 29, 1887.)

Charles H. Utter—trapper, trader, guide, freighter, and miner—a man of many interests, including gambling. (*Scribner's,* September 1872.)

Hunting mule deer in the mountains tested the hunter's skill. (*Scribner's,* September 1872.)

A fisherman's dilemma.
(France, 1887.)

Colorado ranks among the top ten states in variety of up-
land and migratory birds. (Fossett, 1879.)

Colorado attracts vacationers in all seasons. Summer is especially popular with campers.
(Crofutt, 1881.)

Fish and game resources in
Colorado offer sportsmen an
excellent source of recreation
and enjoyment. Furthermore,
in the past decade sportsmen
spent over $50 million
annually.

Climbing Pikes Peak did not deter ladies
in long skirts. (Richardson, 1867.)

Half-way House on the trail to the summit. (*Leslie's*, August 23, 1890.)

Climbers ready to scale Pikes Peak.
(*Leslie's*, August 23, 1890.)

Foothills, mountain parks, and valleys of the high country teemed with antlered American deer, mistakenly called elk. Today, the herds are controlled to prevent overgrazing and starvation. (Crofutt, 1881.)

Bald Eagle, emblem of the American nation. (Ayer, 1880.)

Rocky Mountain quail, winter plumage (left) and summer plumage (right). (*Scribner's*, August 1876.)

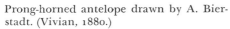

Prong-horned antelope drawn by A. Bierstadt. (Vivian, 1880.)

Coyote, relative of the wolf. (Fossett, 1876.)

Prairie fowl or grouse. (Manning, 1876.)

COW COUNTRY

John Wesley Iliff, the greatest of the Colorado cattle kings, arrived in Denver from Ohio in 1859. Almost immediately he began investing in cattle and by 1868 contracted to supply beef to the Union Pacific railroad crews and guarding troops. At the time of his death in 1878, he owned some 15,000 acres of rangeland from Greeley to Julesburg. (Baskin, 1880.)

WAGON-TRAIN FREIGHTERS were the first to discover the grazing value of the new country. One account states that John D. Henderson, on arrival in Auraria late in 1858, could find no accommodations for his oxen and turned them out on the grass. The following spring, while buffalo hunting, he came upon a well-grazed herd bearing his own brand. In several issues of the *Rocky Mountain News* in December 1859, he advertised his 320-acre ranch on "Henderson Island (in the Platte) . . . for all kinds of stock to winter. . . ."

Cattlemen who owned herds of 10,000 to 50,000 head and corresponding unfenced acreages held sway over the open range, much of which was controlled by English and Scottish interests.

A trail herd fording the South Platte. (Kenderdine, 1888.)

Every cowboy had to take his turn guarding the herd on the night shift. (Thayer, 1887.)

The reign of the cattle kings was brief—scarcely two decades—but supreme while it lasted. Disastrous blizzards, merciless drouth, overstocking of rangeland, and ever-increasing homesteaders' claims all played a major role in the breakdown of individual open-range empires into small-scale fenced ranches with better breeds of stock to replace the Texas Longhorns.

Branding calves always followed the spring roundup. (*Harper's*, November 1879.)

"Come an' Get It!"—the most welcome call from the chuck wagon on roundup or trail drive. (Thayer, 1887.)

Cattlemen and cowboys drove the herds to a designated area, separated the branded cattle, then proceeded to brand the unmarked stock. (Strahorn, 1879.)

Ranch along the Cimarron River in western Colorado shows canvas-topped bunk house, branding corrals, and cowboys at work. (*Harper's Weekly*, April 14, 1888.)

As cattlemen prospered, their ranch houses became more pretentious. This one features a covered but open gallery. (Higgins, 1894.)

Interior views of the Z A Ranch near Colorado Springs—from a collection of original watercolors by Edward Graham Hayes, a cowhand on the ranch from 1886-89. (Western Collection, Colorado State Historical Society.)

SHEPHERDS' KINGDOM

IN SOUTHERN COLORADO sheep arrived with the early Spanish American settlers; however, sheep herding did not develop on a large scale until the early 1870s. Expansion of the railroads resulted in rapid progress, and by 1879 there were almost two million head of sheep in Colorado in spite of the cattlemen's opposition. Although the Western Slope is considered sheep country, toward the end of the century, ranchers in northeastern Colorado gradually began purchasing range lambs to be fattened for market—a branch of animal husbandry which has become very profitable.

Sheepshearing. (Brockett, 1881.)

Morning at a sheep ranch introduces easterners to the rigors of the shepherd's life. (*Harper's,* January 1880.)

Off for the summer range in the mountains.
(*Harper's,* January 1880.)

The sheep industry expanded in spite of the cattlemen's violent opposition, which often resulted in brutal attacks and slaying of herds and herders. (*Harper's Weekly*, October 13, 1877.)

On a road south of Pueblo, death comes to overdriven sheep. (*Illustrated London News*, August 22, 1885.)

A gruesome rendering of the remains of the murdered men. (*Harper's Weekly*, October 17, 1874.)

SINNERS AND SAINTS

IN DECEMBER 1873, a party of Utah prospectors bound for the San Juan Mountains arrived at a Ute encampment. Chief Ouray advised them to remain through the winter; however, six of the men, among them Alfred Packer, decided to continue their journey.

Several weeks later Packer reached the Los Pinos Agency, some seventy miles from Lake City. He claimed to have been deserted by his companions and forced to subsist on roots and small game. Suspicion mounted, and the arrival of an Indian with strips of human flesh he had picked up on the trail resulted in Packer's arrest. The following spring a photographer for *Harper's Weekly* crossed the plateau (now famous as Cannibal Plateau) and stumbled upon the remains of Packer's five companions; and Packer was charged with murder. Despite his protests, and because there was no jail, he was chained to a rock but managed to escape. Ten years later he was caught in Wyoming and returned to Lake City where he was tried and sentenced to hang.

Packer escaped the gallows, and a new trial resulted in a forty-year sentence for manslaughter. Within a few years, however, he was granted a parole and eventually went to Denver where he died in 1906. But in Colorado the taint of cannibalism is still synonymous with his name.

Cannibal Plateau, a few miles from Lake City, scene of a grisly episode in Colorado history. (*Harper's Weekly,* October 17, 1874.)

Burial plots of the five Packer victims. (*Harper's Weekly,* October 17, 1874.)

On the mining frontier only a thin line existed between the law and the lawless. Denver had its share of desperadoes and unscrupulous officials. (*Richardson*, 1867.)

A special agent confronts a pair of outlaws. (*Harper's*, March 1880.)

"I've been looking for you"—six-shooter justice. (*Harper's Weekly, Supplement*, March 28, 1874.)

Running down a thief whose luck has run out. (*Rocky Mountain News*, August, 14, 1898).

The lynching of George R. Witherill at Canon City. (Cook, 1897.)

On the streets of Alamosa the law moves in. (Cook, 1897.)

THE FIVE CENT
WIDE AWAKE
LIBRARY

Entered according to Act of Congress, in the year 18.., by FRANK TOUSEY, in the office of the Librarian of Congress, at Washington, D. C.

Entered at the Post Office at New York, N. Y., as Second Class Matter.

No. 1286 · COMPLETE. · FRANK TOUSEY, PUBLISHER, 34 & 36 NORTH MOORE STREET, N. Y. · PRICE 5 CENTS. · Vol. II
NEW YORK, September 25, 1896. · ISSUED EVERY FRIDAY.

DENVER DAN JR. AND HIS BAND OF DEAD SHOTS
BY "NONAME."

In the dime novel of the day, heroes were good, villains were bad, and the use of the primitivistic motifs in the interpretation of Western American life was an established tradition. In this thriller from *Wide Awake Library,* Denver Dan Jr. and his band of dead shots arrive in the nick of time to thwart a horrible miscarriage of justice. ("Noname," September 25, 1896.)

The Brothers of Light or Penitentes, an offshoot of the Third Order of St. Francis, practiced their rites in New Mexico and southern Colorado. The *sangrader,* leader of the group, used a flint to cut the seal of the order upon the back of the initiate. (Darley, 1893.)

A whip and a flint used to discipline the body. (Darley, 1893.)

The Way of the Cross led to the local calvary. The procession—hooded cross-bearing victims accompanied by the whippers, the reader, and the flute player whose eerie wail pierced the night with a haunting dirge. (Darley, 1893.)

AGRICULTURE

Land promoters magnified the pleasures of hand irrigating. (Thayer, 1887.)

IN THE 1870s the fertile valleys of the South Platte and the Cache la Poudre beckoned organized colonies to Greeley and Longmont, and to Fort Collins, Berthoud, and Loveland.

In the 1880s, in the Arkansas Valley, eastward from Pueblo, extensive irrigation systems reached to Lamar and Holly. In this extreme eastern portion of the state, as the valleys gave way to the prairies, homesteaders responded to the offer of free land in the areas that became Sterling, Akron, Yuma, and Wray.

Countless foreigners who read the railroad pamphlets glorifying the wide open spaces of the West gathered a few belongings and booked passage to the United States. Many of these emigrants worked in coal mines to earn enough money for a down payment on land.

The big agricultural boom that resulted caused the Great American Desert, in the words of the prophet Isaiah, to "blossom as the rose."

"Lifting wheels" on the Gunnison River raised water to sluices for passage to ditches and fields. (*Harper's Weekly*, November 20, 1886.)

"Ditch-riders" opening a headgate to allow water to run into a sluiceway. (*Harper's Weekly*, June 20, 1874.)

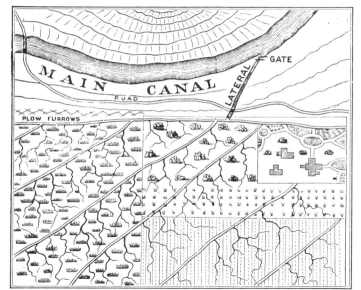

Water was never wasted. Map shows how the water was diverted, stored, and distributed to the fields of thirsting crops. (Thayer, 1887.)

THE SPANISH AMERICAN pioneers in the San Luis Valley began irrigation of small crops in the 1850s. Large-scale irrigation developed in 1870 when the Union Colony at Greeley, inspired by the vision of Horace Greeley, dug the first canal.

Irrigation is very important in the semi-arid sections of Colorado that do not receive the required twenty inches of rainfall for crop production. (Western Collection, Colorado State Historical Society.)

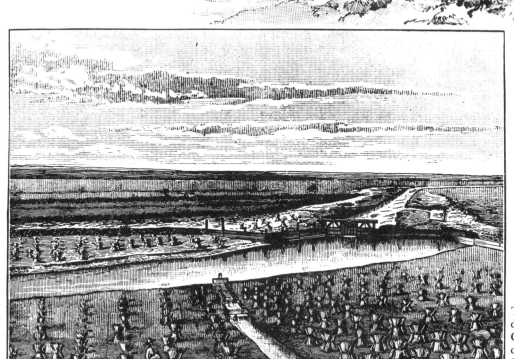

The San Luis People's Ditch, dug in 1852 by the settlers on Culebra Creek, is the oldest in continuous use. (*City of Pueblo*, 1890.)

Not all the fifty-niners found their treasure in the mines. Many who cleared land in the valleys stretching to the edges of the plains found that the earth also yielded riches. By the end of the century Colorado's greatest source of wealth lay in agriculture. (Williams, 1891.)

Like a flotilla of river paddlewheelers, binders cut through the sea of grain. (Brockett, 1881.)

In 1861, M. C. Fisher brought the first threshing machine to the Platte Valley. (Thayer, 1887.)

Before 1870 the plains Indians were alternately hostile and friendly toward settlers. Devastation of isolated farms and settlements was fairly common until the battles of Beecher Island (1868) and Summit Springs (1869) which resulted in removal of the Indians. (Clampitt, 1889.)

The early farmer faced many hardships—flooding rains, drouth, dust, hail, and blizzards—but the most destructive were the ravaging hordes of grasshoppers. (Richardson, 1867.)

The disk harrow preparing the soil for planting. (Thayer, 1887.)

EASTERN VALLEY TOWNS

LONGMONT, a semi-cooperative colony, organized by the Chicago-Colorado Colony Company, was established in 1871 with the arrival of 400 settlers. Named for the peak which dominates the western horizon, it has always been considered the most typical rural American town in the state.

The Bryant School.
(*Longmont Times,* October 4, 1892.)

THE AREA from Boulder northward to Fort Collins and Greeley soon became known as one of the most productive agricultural regions in the state. With the advent of the Model T it also became a tourist attraction.

Methodist church and parsonage. *Longmont Times,* October 4, 1892.)

J. B. Adams's apiary, Boulder County. A "buzzing" business which led to the celebration of Honey Day in 1892. (*Longmont Times,* October 4, 1892.)

City Hall. (*Longmont Times,* October, 4, 1892.)

LOVELAND, named for W. A. H. Loveland, promoter of the Colorado Central Railroad, is in the heart of this prosperous area. Before the cherry orchards and the St. Valentine's Day postal service made Loveland famous, its boast was "corn, ten-feet high," and a free-feed Corn Roast Day inaugurated in 1894.

Farm and residence of Alfred Wild who, in the early 1880s, built the first plaster mill in the state. (*Fort Collins Express,* 1894.)

Berthoud Farmers' Mill and Elevator. Berthoud was named for Captain Edward L. Berthoud, Civil War officer and railroad construction engineer, and is the oldest community in the Little Big Thompson Valley. Surrounded by green fields, its solid homes and beautiful flower gardens reflect the character of the people. (*Fort Collins Express,* 1894.)

The first settlement (1864-71) on the site of Fort Collins was a military post, named for Lt. William O. Collins at Fort Laramie, to protect settlers in the Cache la Poudre and to guard the Overland Trail. In 1873, General Robert A. Cameron formed a town company similar to the colony towns. The settlers were determined, for even two grasshopper tornados in 1875 and 1876 did not daunt them. Within a decade the area and the town (shown as it looked in 1899) with its wide streets and grain and (at the turn of the century) the standing production center for livestock and grain and (at the turn of the century) the sugar beet industry. (Western Collection, Denver Public Library.)

In 1870, territorial legislation nominally created a State Agricultural College at Fort Collins as a land-grant college under the Morrill Act. To many it was absurd that a school for agricultural science should be located in the Great American Desert with its dry prairies, bleached buffalo bones, and coyotes. (*Fort Collins Express*, 1894.)

Lack of funds and land donations by citizens delayed the opening of the Colorado State College of Agriculture and Mechanic Arts until 1879. But the desert, the buffalo bones, and the coyotes gave way to a beautiful campus; and the college that was a joke in 1870 has become the present-day Colorado State University with an enviable reputation as an agricultural institution. (*Longmont Times*, October 4, 1892.)

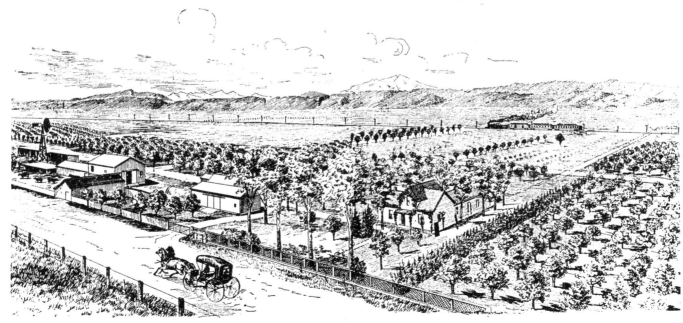

Fossil Creek Fruit Farm owned by J. S. McClelland. Fossils of prehistoric fish have been found along the creek. (*Fort Collins Express*, 1894.)

Interior of F. P. Stover's drug store on Main Street. (*Fort Collins Express*, 1894.)

For rent at J. H. Gault's livery: buggies, carriages, carts, and high-stepping teams. (*Fort Collins Express*, 1894.)

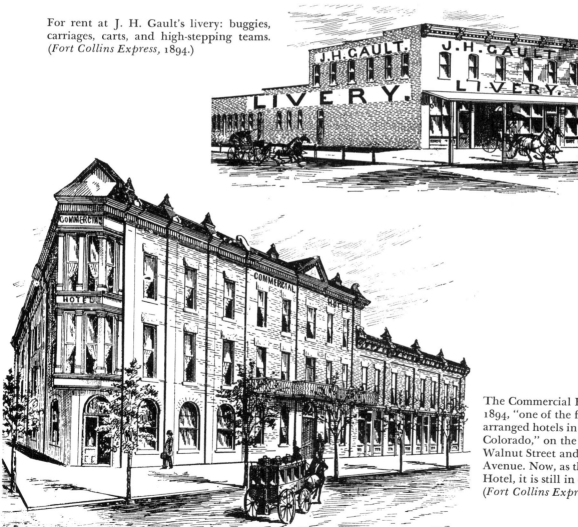

The Commercial Hotel, built in 1894, "one of the finest and best arranged hotels in northern Colorado," on the corner of Walnut Street and College Avenue. Now, as the Northern Hotel, it is still in operation. (*Fort Collins Express*, 1894.)

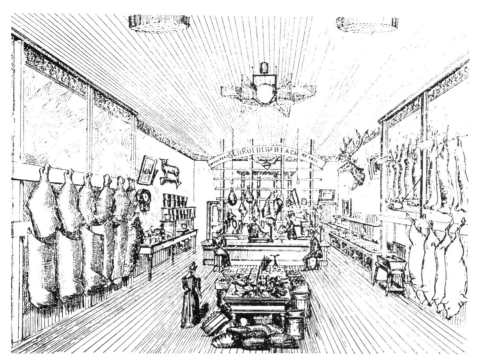

AT FIRST cattle and hogs were the mainstay of the livestock industry. Sheep raising developed slowly in the early 1880s, but within a decade was displaced by lamb fattening; and Fort Collins became one of the largest centers of lamb processing in America. Early in the 1900s Lamb Day is celebrated annually with a free barbecue for some 10,000 people.

Interior of Schroeder & Beach's, a wholesale and retail meat market. (*Fort Collins Express*, 1894.)

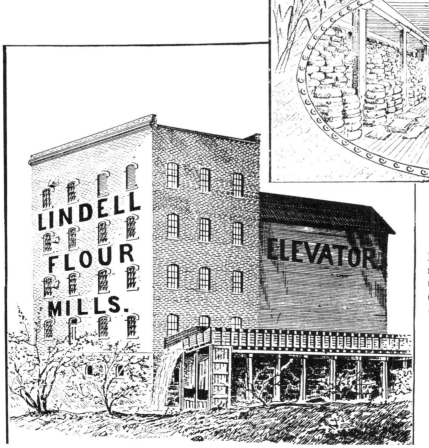

In the towns of the wheat-raising communities, flour was very expensive before the advent of flour mills such as Lindell's (interior and exterior shown). (*Fort Collins Express*, 1894.)

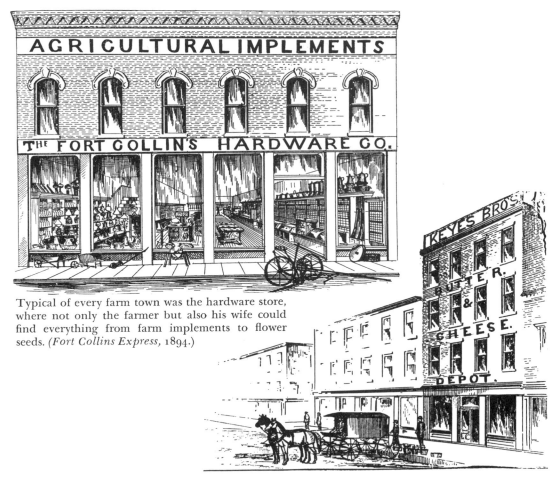

Typical of every farm town was the hardware store, where not only the farmer but also his wife could find everything from farm implements to flower seeds. (*Fort Collins Express*, 1894.)

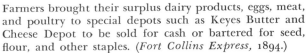

Farmers brought their surplus dairy products, eggs, meat, and poultry to special depots such as Keyes Butter and Cheese Depot to be sold for cash or bartered for seed, flour, and other staples. (*Fort Collins Express*, 1894.)

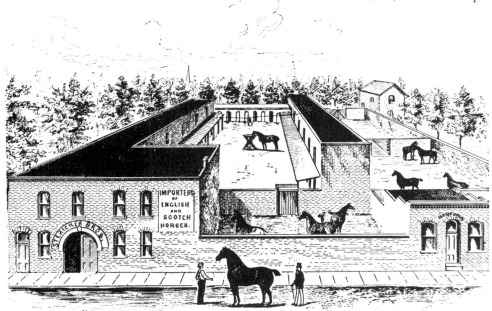

Stericker Brothers' Stable—the Fort Collins branch of the Pickering, England, and Springfield, Illinois, establishment that imported fine English and Scottish horses. (*Fort Collins Express*, 1894.)

THE UNION COLONY, a cooperative agricultural enterprise, was organized under the enthusiastic leadership of Nathan C. Meeker, agricultural editor of Horace Greeley's *New York Tribune*. Meeker, with Robert A. Cameron and Richmond Fisk, selected a site along the Cache la Poudre and founded Greeley, so named for the famous editor, in 1870.

Union Bank, built in 1888. (*Colorado's Enterprising Cities,* 1893.)

Nathan Meeker became an Indian agent at the White River Agency, the site of an Indian massacre in which he and his associates were murdered. Meeker's portrait and residence are shown. (Thayer, 1887.)

General Robert A. Cameron, one of the founders of Greeley. Like several towns in the state, Greeley was called "The Garden City of Colorado." (Boyd, 1890.)

Greeley Opera House, considered the finest north of Denver. (Boyd, 1890.)

In 1890, to provide Weld County with better qualified teachers, state legislators appropriated $10,000 to help build a normal school at Greeley. The county cooperated with 40 acres of land and $15,000, only to learn that the state could not meet its commitment. Bent on having better teachers, citizens of Weld County raised the money and got their school in 1890. Later as the Colorado State College of Education (1935), and more recently (1970) as the University of Northern Colorado, it is one of the leading teacher training institutions in the country. (Denver and Rio Grande Railroad, 1898.)

Residence of Governor Benjamin H. Eaton who built one of the earliest irrigation ditches in the region. (Boyd, 1890.)

The Oasis Hotel, the scene of many social affairs, was no hangout for liquor lovers. The absence of saloons, variety halls, pool rooms, and brothels in Greeley led outsiders to refer to the residents as "Greeley Saints." (Boyd, 1890.)

The main street of Akron, 1888. No branch of agriculture tested man's endurance as much as "dry farming." Western states offered no aid to the homesteaders who took up claims in the range country; but being land hungry they were determined to wrest a living from the prairie soil. In the following century agricultural colleges, experiment stations, and extension programs helped to solve their problems. (Western Collection, Colorado State Historical Society.)

Lamar, the youngest city in the Arkansas Valley, was founded in 1886 by L. Q. C. Lamar, Secretary of the Interior under President Grover Cleveland. (Denver & Rio Grande Railroad, 1898.)

The ranch headquarters of the H. S. Holly Company which ran cattle west and north in 1870s. At Holly, the first Colorado town west on the Santa Fe Trail, easterners caught their first glimpse of the Rockies. (Baskin, 1881.)

MOUNTAIN PARKS

IN 1859, JOEL ESTES was the first white man to look upon the peaceful secluded area that became Estes Park.

Excellent illustration of granite foliation. (*Hand-Book of Colorado,* 1879.)

Longs Peak lava beds. (Bishop, 1879-80.)

Estes Park. In 1873, Rocky Mountain Jim (James Nugent), a trapper, guided Isabella L. Bird, an English author, on horseback travels in the area, which she delightfully reported in *A Lady's Life in the Rocky Mountains.* (Vivian, 1880.)

"Longs Peak from Estes Park," one of Thomas Moran's well-known landscapes of the West. (Crofutt, 1881.)

In the center of the state, from north to south behind the front ranges, are three beautiful valleys encircled by snow-capped mountains. Here the Indian and buffalo roamed; and trappers, following streams that abounded with beaver, heard only the heartbeat of the wilderness.

In North Park, where the North Platte begins, fur companies held sway in the 1820s and 1830s. John C. Frémont, the explorer, passed through in the 1840s; and in 1855 Sir George Gore, an Irish nobleman, with Jim Bridger as guide, went on a hunting party that amounted to wanton slaughter. After a brief attraction for miners, this valley which Frémont described as "a paradise to all grazing animals" was finally discovered by stockmen.

Although named by Frémont in the 1840s, for nearly a century Middle Park on the Grand River (shown in sketch) was not formally a part of the United States. In 1936, in a ceremony at Breckenridge, Governor Edwin C. Johnson raised the American flag and finally claimed Middle Park as a part of Colorado. (Kansas Pacific Railroad, 1875.)

North Park extends into Wyoming. In 1876 Wyoming built a road to connect North Park with the outside world. Later a toll road from Fort Collins over Cameron Pass reached Teller. Charles Boettcher, pioneer merchant, and his partners established the Big Horn Ranch which eventually extended over 22,000 acres. (Vivian, 1880.)

SOUTH, ACROSS THE CONTINENTAL DIVIDE is Middle Park where the Colorado River flows westward to the Pacific, and clear streams wind through grassy plains. Gore also invaded this area, then headed west across the range that bears his name. In 1864, W. N. Byers (publisher of the *Rocky Mountain News*) used Indian scrip to purchase the townsite of Hot Sulphur Springs from a squaw; a decade later Lord Dunraven, a British peer, bagged hundreds of game animals. Grand Lake, the popular tourist town, began as an outfitting station for prospectors lured by the rumors of gold and silver in the Never Summer Mountains.

South Park, a broad mountain meadow at the source of the South Platte, may, according to geological surveys, once have been an inland sea. Pike explored here in 1806; Frémont reported on the abundance of wild life; and the Englishman, George Frederick Ruxton, traveled through in 1847 and recorded his impressions in *Life in the Far West*. A short-lived gold rush created the towns of Tarryall and Fairplay before the cattlemen and ranchers took over.

Grand Crater near Longs Peak. This illustration appears in the book by Isabella Bird, *A Lady's Life in the Rocky Mountains*. (Bishop, 1879-80.)

South Park on the eastern slope of the continental divide was, according to geologists, once a seabed. The trappers called it *bayou salado* (salt marsh). (Rusling, 1874.)

PUEBLO—
"PITTSBURGH OF THE WEST"

INDIANS, MEXICANS, and explorers had long been familiar with Old Fort Pueblo at the junction of the Arkansas and Fountain rivers, a winter rendezvous for trappers and traders. In 1854, the Utes, under the influence of whiskey, instigated the Christmas Day Massacre—slaying every white man on the spot. Present-day Pueblo began that same year when rival groups settled on either side of Fountain Creek. The east side, called Pueblo, won over Independence on the west.

Mexican interior. Francis Parkman, a historian from Boston, described the interior of the state apartment of the Pueblo as "a small mud room, very neatly furnished, considering the material, and garnished with a crucifix, a looking-glass, a picture of the Virgin, and a rusty horse-pistol. . . ." (*Lippincott's,* December 1880.)

Houses of adobe brick are characteristic of southern Colorado and New Mexico. (*Harper's Weekly,* May 12, 1888.)

On lower Santa Fe Avenue, early in 1860, Colonel Albert Boone, nephew of Daniel, opened the first general store in Pueblo. (*Lippincott's,* December 1880.)

A bird's-eye view of Pueblo, South Pueblo, and East Pueblo, which illustrates the phenomenal growth of the area following the arrival of the Denver & Rio Grande Railroad in 1872 and the Atchison, Topeka & Santa Fe four years later. By the 1880s, Pueblo had steel mills, smelters, and railroad roundhouses, as well as flour mills. In one decade the population increased from 3,217 to 24,588. (Crofutt, 1881.)

Pueblo's Opera House, with a seating capacity of 1,500, constructed in 1890 at the corner of Fourth and Main streets. As a member of Tabor's Silver Circuit which brought opera companies from the East and abroad, Pueblo could offer its music lovers the best in grand opera. (*Colorado's Enterprising Cities,* 1893.)

Colorado State Hospital for the Insane was established in 1879. Housed originally in the mansion of George M. Chilcott, former delegate to Congress from the Colorado Territory, it has expanded into a notable institution. (*Harper's Weekly,* May 12, 1888.)

Union Depot on South Union Avenue. (*Colorado's Enterprising Cities,* 1893.)

In 1880, William J. Palmer merged three of his enterprises into the Colorado Coal and Iron Company which turned out the first steel west of the Mississippi River. After a second merger in 1892 it became the Colorado Fuel and Iron Company—until World War II the largest in the West. (*Colorado's Enterprising Cities,* 1893.)

PUEBLO, second largest city in the state and center of trade and industry in southern Colorado, is the site of the Colorado State Fair. The Fair, established in 1887, is held annually in late August. Today, Pueblo, a highly industrialized city, keeps up with educational, cultural, and recreational innovations.

In 1882, Central High School replaced the first school building in South Pueblo. (*Harper's Weekly*, May 12, 1888.)

City Hall. (*Colorado's Enterprising Cities*, 1893.)

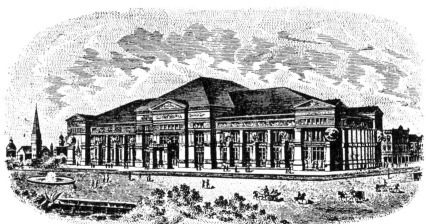

The Mineral Palace in Mineral Park, between 15th and 19th streets, housed one of the most complete collections of minerals in the United States. To publicize Colorado as a mining state, the Mineral Palace had a gala opening on July 4, 1890. (*Colorado's Enterprising Cities*, 1893.)

The Spanish Peaks, dominating the horizon south of Walsenburg, were to the Indians and the Spanish—*huajatolla*, the breasts of the world. (Frémont, 1887.)

Bank in Trinidad, on the north fork of the Purgatoire River. The name *purgatoire* is an example of the influence of French and other tongues on the region. Spanish explorers had named the river *El Rio de las Animas Perdidas en Purgatorio* (river of lost souls in purgatory); French trappers shortened it to Purgatoire, from which American cowboys derived "Picketwire." (*Colorado's Enterprising Cities,* 1893.)

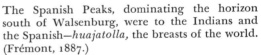

Spanish explorers, Mexican American farmers, traders, and trappers took part in the history of Walsenburg and Trinidad. The name of the Unfug brothers, general merchants, is also etched deep in the history of the community. (*Colorado's Enterprising Cities,* 1893.)

ROYAL GORGE AREA

Royal Gorge Hot Springs Hotel and Mineral Baths. In his journal Pike states that the springs are "strongly impregnated with sulphur." (*Colorado's Enterprising Cities*, 1893.)

THE SITE OF CANON CITY near the entrance to the Royal Gorge was well known to the Utes. Here Zebulon M. Pike built a blockhouse in January 1807 and later moved south to the San Luis Valley. The rush of 1859 brought men up the Arkansas to this inviting spot; and Canon City, established in 1860, became a supply center for the mines in California Gulch near the headwaters of the Arkansas.

Canon City in the 1870s. In the foreground (left) is the high-walled Colorado State Penitentiary. (*Fremont and Custer Counties*, 1879.)

The Royal Gorge, also called the Grand Canyon of the Arkansas, where red granite walls rise more than 1,000 feet above the river. The highest suspension bridge in the world crosses this famous gorge. (*Fremont and Custer Counties,* 1879.)

Fremont County Court House. On June 24, 1861, County Judge John Howard divorced his wife by issuing a quit-claim on her. He wrote, it is said, "She . . . may in the future be claimed under squatter title." (Baskin, 1881.)

In January 1868, the Colorado State Penitentiary in Canon City was established by legislative action, and the first cell building opened in 1871. Prison labor included dressing stone, making bricks, as well as the maintenance of buildings, farm, and garden. (Baskin, 1881.)

A Colorado Stage and Express Company daily coach which left Canon City at 7:30 a.m. arrived at Rosita and Silver Cliff approximately eight hours later. (*Fremont and Custer Counties,* 1879.)

The daily stage passed through Hungry Gulch, a small mining camp of log cabins, en route to Rosita and Silver Cliff. (*Harper's,* February 1880.)

Silver Cliff, bonanza town, named for the massive silver-bearing cliff it faces. By 1881, with an estimated population in excess of 5,000, it was the third largest city in Colorado. (*Harper's,* February 1880.)

In Rosita, a typical rough mining camp established in 1870, claim jumping among the lawless ended in gunplay. Here Carl Wulsten, German promoter, died in poverty. (*Harper's,* February 1880.)

Carl Wulsten, leader of the colony sponsored by the German Coloniza-tion Society. (Baskin, 1881.)

A road station in Wet Mountain Valley, the scene of settle-ment by the German Colonization Society. (Campion, 1878.)

Departure of German emigrants from Chicago, bound for "Colfax, Colorado Territory." (*Harper's Weekly,* March 26, 1870.)

WESTERN SLOPE

THE WESTERN SLOPE was Colorado's last frontier. In the northwest area, once a wilderness known only to trappers and cattle rustlers, the impact of development was not felt until the new century.

In the 1870s, with the discovery of gold in the San Juan Mountains, mountain and valley echoed the demand, "The Utes must go!" When the ultimatum was finally issued in 1881, development came in one great stride, not through mining, but through orchards, farms, and ranches. The Uteland which travelers and reporters had likened to the Sahara Desert became, within a decade, a gigantic fruit basket—one of the best in the nation.

In tribute to this miracle, Grand Junction, destined to become the nation's uranium capital and the largest city on the Western Slope, inaugurated its first Peach Day in 1891. In a pavilion on the fair grounds (with "rest cots available"), the people listened to effulgent oratory, viewed the lush fruit display, then sat down to a free lunch "with all the peaches you can eat . . . and may the Lord preserve you from cholera morbus!"

The Black Canyon of the Gunnison River is one of the most majestic and spectacular gorges. The beauty of its color is best revealed when sunshine penetrates the cavernous depth. (*Cosmopolitan,* March 1888.)

Lake City, one of the first settlements on the west slope. According to various accounts, the first words of Arthur Chapman, famous for his poem "Out Where the West Begins," when he visited Lake City were, "I have found where the West begins!" (Fossett, 1879.)

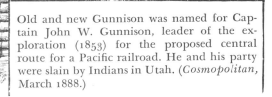

Old and new Gunnison was named for Captain John W. Gunnison, leader of the exploration (1853) for the proposed central route for a Pacific railroad. He and his party were slain by Indians in Utah. (*Cosmopolitan,* March 1888.)

Coke from Crested Butte was used in smelters and later in steel and iron manufacture. By 1890 there were 916 coke ovens in Colorado. (*Cosmopolitan*, March 1888.)

The razor-edged crest of Italian Mountain (13,255 ft.), east of Crested Butte. Ore was mined in this district early in the twentieth century. (Tenney, 1880.)

Crested Butte, a coal mining community (mine and breakers shown), began as a gold mining camp in the early 1880s. During the 1870s and the 1880s coal brought two dollars per ton at the mines. (*Cosmopolitan*, March 1888.)

Conditions in the coal mines were wretched and dangerous. Gas and dust explosions were a constant threat. A disaster at the Crested Butte mines in the early 1880s took several lives. (*Harper's Weekly*, February 16, 1884.)

Crested Butte Mountain and Lake. (Wood, 1889.)

Gothic, ten miles north of Crested Butte, boomed in 1881 with the discovery of sylvanite—a native telluride approximately 24.5 percent gold and 13.4 percent silver. Thousands of miners searched for this precious metal. (*Cosmopolitan*, March 1888.)

First National Bank at Montrose, the trading center of a rich agricultural region. The uranium ores used by Mme. Marie Curie, who discovered pure radium, came from western Montrose County. (Denver & Rio Grande Railroad, 1898.)

From Montrose south to Ouray, travelers passed through the grassy Uncompahgre Valley. (*Cosmopolitan*, March 1888.)

The Uncompahgre Valley proved ideal for farming and stock raising. (*Harper's Weekly*, April 14, 1888.)

Bird's-eye view of Ouray. Mines such as Yankee Boy, Trout, Johnny Bull, and Fisherman were close to Ouray; Hidden Treasure, Millionaire, Hoosier Girl, and many others in the Imogene Basin and on Mt. Sneffles made Ouray famous in the 1880s. The Camp Bird mine, also in this area, produced a fortune in 1896 for Thomas F. Walsh, one-time owner of the Hope diamond. (Denver & Rio Grande Railroad, 1896.)

The precipitous stage road to Red Mountain where the largest mines— the Yankee Girl and the Guston— operated until 1896. (*Cosmopolitan*, March 1888.)

Map of the San Juan mining district. (Bancroft, 1890.)

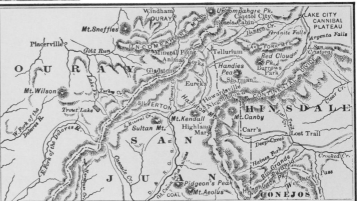

Sultan Mountain (13,341 ft.), a great sentinel southwest of Silverton, the San Juan County seat. (*Harper's,* April 1882.)

Silverton, originally Baker's Park. Legend says it was renamed when a miner remarked, "We may not have gold here, but we have silver by the ton." (*Harper's,* April 1882.)

King Solomon Mountain, north of Silverton. (*Harper's,* April 1882.)

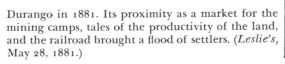

Durango in 1881. Its proximity as a market for the mining camps, tales of the productivity of the land, and the railroad brought a flood of settlers. (*Leslie's,* May 28, 1881.)

In 1878 Ophir Gulch—dominated by Mt. Wilson (14,246 ft.) and located on the South Fork of the San Miguel River—became an important mining camp. (*Harper's,* April 1882.)

Winter in the San Juan Mountains complicated life for the miners—heavy snows, severe cold, and avalanches frequently marooned them for weeks. (Fossett, 1879.)

Rico, visited by the Spanish and mountain men, was in the possession of the Utes until they surrendered their lands in 1873. As late as the 1920s, it was a haven for horse thieves who were being pursued by posses in automobiles and on motorcycles. (*Harpers,* April 1882.)

Timber bridges constructed over ravines made the high country accessible for pack trains. (*Cosmopolitan,* March 1888.)

Northwest of Montrose the stage reached Delta, where Antoine Robidoux, a French trapper, built a fort in 1830. Delta is one of the state's largest fruit growing areas. (*Cosmopolitan,* March 1888.)

MESAS AND PLATEAUS are common in much of the western slope area. Plateau country, although rich in oil shale deposits, offers little land for cultivation; however, the valleys are adaptable to agriculture and grazing.

The canyon of the Uncompahgre River. (Fossett, 1879.)

Rock sculpture on the White River illustrates centuries of natural geologic erosion. (*Fremont and Custer Counties,* 1879.)

FEASTS AND FESTIVALS

COLORADO WAS and still is a celebrating state. In the last two decades of the nineteenth century, Coloradoans became festival mad; and, said the editor of the *Denver Times,* "the state comes pretty near being a festival three hundred and sixty-five days in the calendar year."

Denver showed her appreciation for blessings counted with the Festival of Mountain and Plain in a week-long celebration. Elsewhere there were the Blossom Festival in Canon City, the Flower Festival in Colorado Springs, and even a three-day jack rabbit "hunting expedition" to Lamar to bring back the kill for Denver's poor. Denver also staged the last great feast "on the wild meat of the plains" to honor the 1898 National Livestock Convention. A crowd of 30,000 dined free and freely on buffalo, elk, bear, antelope, beaver, sheep, and opossum— and drank 300 kegs of beer.

A Potato Bake and Barbecue at Monument in November of 1889 and 1890 failed because of inclement weather. Rescheduled for September in following years, it attracted several thousand visitors. (*Rocky Mountain News,* September 23, 1891.)

George W. Swink originated the Rocky Ford Watermelon Day in 1878. By 1891, with 8,000 visitors including Governor John L. Routt and with 10,000 melons, it was a grand success. This festival is still celebrated due to Swink's foresight; he deeded land to the fairgrounds with the condition that Melon Day be observed. (*Rocky Mountain News,* September 4, 1891.)

Denver's Festival of Mountain and Plain, inaugurated in October, 1895, was an optimistic sign that the city had recovered from the panic of 1893. It was held annually through 1899 and revived in 1901 and 1912. For one week Denver, in the fashion of Mardi Gras at New Orleans, was a scene of gay abandon with elaborate balls, parties, street dancing, and parades.

Arapahoe County float illustrating agricultural, mining, and commercial progress in Denver's 1896 Festival of Mountain and Plain. (*Rocky Mountain News,* October 7, 1896.)

Float representing the leading mining interests of the state in Denver's 1896 Festival of Mountain and Plain. (*Rocky Mountain News,* October 7, 1896.)

COWBOY CONTESTS took place as early as 1869. Sometimes called tournaments, they were features of various celebrations in the 1880s and 1890s. These contests, the forerunners of modern rodeo, anticipated by a decade the public acclaim showered on Cheyenne's Frontier Days. Headquarters for the Rodeo Cowboys' Association is in Denver.

Steer riding. (*Denver Republican*, October 15, 1891.)

One of Roosevelt's Rough Riders with an "ornery bronc." (*Rocky Mountain News*, August 14, 1898.)

Roping a steer at the Denver Exposition, 1887. (*Denver Republican*, October 15, 1887.)

In 1895, a period of prosperity in Leadville, businessmen conceived the Crystal Carnival to attract tourists. The Ice Palace, the main feature of the carnival, was a castle-like structure that covered nearly five acres. Inside were a skating rink, ballroom, restaurant, and shops. The various products of the state—fruit, vegetables, meat, ores, and so forth—were frozen into the 8-foot-thick walls. A bizarre undertaking since both thaw and bitter cold threatened it, the palace lasted until it was declared unsafe in July 1896. (Western Collection, Colorado State Historical Society.)

The most popular and long lasting were the food festivals which continued on a much larger scale to the twentieth century. The earliest was Watermelon Day in Rocky Ford, and like prairie fire the idea spread to other areas: Peach Day in Grand Junction, Potato Day in Monument and Greeley, Strawberry Day in Glenwood Springs, Fish Fry Day in Gunnison, and Corn Day in Loveland.

Thousands journeyed by special passenger train, tallyho, horse and buggy, wagon, and bicycle to a "free feast that would bring tears of joy to the eyes of a patent medicine man with remedies for indigestion."

Denver celebrated the completion of the Denver, Texas and Gulf Railroad with a jubilee in March 1888. (*Leslie's,* April 21, 1888.)

ACKNOWLEDGMENTS

THE GOODWILL AND TALENTS of many individuals lightened the preparation of *Picturesque Colorado,* and to them I am most grateful.

At the University of Colorado: Dr. Ralph E. Ellsworth, Director of Libraries, gave carte blanche access to all resources: Professors Fritz L. Hoffman and Daniel M. Smith, chairmen of the Department of History, graciously reduced my teaching load; Professor Robert G. Athearn suggested my name as author to the publisher. Under the direction of Dr. John A. Brennan, Curator of the Western Historical Collection, S. Kay Evatz and Mrs. Sandra V. Tiberio patiently hauled out volumes and hunted for elusive illustrations. In the Photo Duplication Department, Doris E. Dunkelberger and Mary C. Wing efficiently produced copies of innumerable illustrations.

Staff members of the Colorado State Historical Society and in the Western Collection of the Denver Public Library devoted priceless time to further search, endless aid, and valuable suggestions. At the former, special acknowledgment is due Miss Maxine Benson, State Historian, and Mrs. Enid T. Thompson, Librarian; at the latter, Mrs. Alys Freeze, Mr. James H. Davis and Mrs. Hazel Lundberg.

Mr. Gil L. Campbell, United States Air Force Academy, permitted me to peruse his personal collection of 19th century illustrations and enlightened me in the many intricacies of reproducing engravings, lithographs, wood-cuts, sketches, et cetera.

The dedication to my wife Thérèse reflects only in part my gratitude, for she not only lent moral support but also helped immeasurably in the preparation.

BIBLIOGRAPHY

Abert, Lt. James W. *Report of an Expedition . . . On the Upper Arkansas.* Washington: 1845.

Ayer, I. Winslow. *Life in the Wilds of America.* Grand Rapids: 1880.

Bancroft, Hubert Howe. *History of Nevada, Colorado and Wyoming, 1540-1888.* San Francisco: 1890.

Barnes, J. K. *A Report on the Hygiene of the U. S. Army.* Washington: 1875.

Baskin, O. L., and Company, publisher. *History of Clear Creek and Boulder Valleys.* Chicago: 1880.

Baskin, O. L., and Company, publisher. *History of the City of Denver, Arapahoe County, and Colorado.* Chicago: 1880.

Baskin, O. L., and Company, publisher. *History of the Arkansas Valley, Colorado.* Chicago: 1881.

Beadle, J. H. *The Undeveloped West.* Philadelphia: 1873.

Beaugrand, Honoré. *Six-Mois Dans Les Montagnes-Rocheuses.* Montreal: 1890.

Beckwith, Edward Griffin. *Upon the Route Near the Thirty-eight and Thirty-ninth Parallel.* Washington: 1855.

Beckwourth, James P. *My Life and Adventures.* New York: 1856.

Bishop, Isabella L. B. *A Lady's Life in the Rocky Mountains.* New York: 1879-1880.

Boyd, David. *A History of the Union Colony of Colorado.* Greeley: 1890.

Brockett, Linus Pierpont. *Our Western Empire: or the New West Beyond the Mississippi.* Philadelphia: 1881.

Buckman, G. R. *Colorado Springs, Colorado and Its Famous Scenic Environs.* Colorado Springs: 1892-1893.

Byers, William N., and Kellom, John H. *Hand Book to the Gold Fields of Nebraska and Kansas.* Chicago: 1859.

Campion, J. S. *On the Frontier.* London: 1878.

Century Illustrated Monthly Magazine. New York: 1891.

Clampitt, John Wesley. *Echoes from the Rocky Mountains.* Chicago: 1889.

Colorado A Guide to the Highest State (American Guide Series) . New York: 1941.

Conard, Howard Louis. *Uncle Dick Wootton.* Chicago: 1890.

Cook, David J. *Hands Up.* Denver: 1897.

Cosmopolitan Magazine. New York: 1888.

Crofutt, George A. *Grip-Sack Guide of Colorado.* Omaha: 1881.

Daily Colorado Tribune. Denver: 1870.

Darley, Alex M. *The Passionists of the Southwest.* Pueblo: 1893.

Denver and Rio Grande Railroad. *Rhymes of the Rockies.* Chicago: 1891.

Denver and Rio Grande Railroad. *Slopes of the Sangre de Cristo.* Denver: 1898.

Denver and Rio Grande Railroad. *Tourists' Hand-Book.* Chicago: 1896.

Denver Real Estate and Stock Exchange. Denver: 1891-1892.

Denver Republican. Denver: 1887, 1888.

Dodge, Richard Irving. *The Hunting Grounds of the Great West.* London: 1878.

Drake, Samuel Adams. *The Making of the Great West.* New York: 1887.

Dunn, Jacob Piatt, Jr. *Massacres of the Mountains.* New York: 1886.

Ellis, Edwards S. *The Indian Wars of the United States.* Grand Rapids: 1892.

Ferris, George T. *Our Native Land.* New York: 1886.

Fort Collins Express, Industrial Edition. Fort Collins: 1894.

Fossett, Frank. *Colorado, Its Gold and Silver Mines.* New York: 1876, 1879.

France, Lewis B. *Mountain Trails and Parks in Colorado.* Denver: 1887.

Frank Leslie's Illustrated Newspaper. New York: 1859, 1860, 1879, 1881, 1888, 1890.

Fremont, John Charles. *Memoirs of My Life.* V. 1. Chicago and New York: 1887.

Georgetown Courier. *Among the Silver Seams of Colorado.* Georgetown: 1886.

Greatorex, Eliza. *Summer Etchings in Colorado.* New York: 1873.

Griswold, Don and Jean. *Colorado's Century of "Cities."* Denver: 1958.

Hafen, Le Roy R. (ed.) *Colorado and Its People.* New York: 1948.

Hall, Frank. *History of the State of Colorado.* v. 3. Chicago: 1891.

Hand-Book of Colorado. Denver: 1879.

Hand Book to the Gold Fields . . . see: Byers.

Harper's Monthly Magazine. New York: 1853-1897.

Harper's Weekly. New York: 1866-1894.

Hayes, A. A. *New Colorado and the Santa Fe Trail.* New York: 1880.

Higgins, Charles A. *New Guide to the Pacific Coast.* Chicago and New York: 1894.

Historical and Descriptive of Fremont and Custer Counties with their Principal Towns. Canon City: 1879.

Historical Descriptive Review of Colorado's Enterprising Cities. Denver: 1893.

Hughes, John Taylor. *Doniphan's Expedition.* Cincinnati: 1848.

Illustrated London News. 1877-1887.

Ingersoll, Ernest. *Knocking Round the Rockies.* New York: 1883.

Ingham, G. Thomas. *Digging Gold Among the Rockies.* Philadelphia: 1880.

Jackson, Helen Hunt. *Bits of Travel at Home.* Boston: 1878.

Kansas Pacific Railroad. *Rocky Mountain Resorts.* Chicago: 1875.

Kenderdine, Thaddeus S. *A California Tramp.* Newton, Pa.: 1888.

Leadville, Lake County and the Gold Belt. Denver: 1895.

Le Tour Du Monde, v. 17. (1869)

Leslie's: see *Frank Leslie's*

Lippincott's Magazine. Philadelphia: 1880-1883.

Longmont Times, Honey Day Edition. October 4, 1892.

Ludlow, Fitz Hugh. *The Heart of the Continent.* New York: 1870.

Marcy, Capt. Randolph. *The Prairie Traveler: a Handbook for Overland Expeditions.* New York: 1859.

Manning, Samuel, Rev. *American Pictures.* London: 1876.

Mathews, Alfred E. *Canyon City, Colorado, and Its Surroundings.* New York: 1870.

Mathews, Alfred E. *Gems of Rocky Mountain Scenery.* New York: 1868-1869.

Mathews, Alfred E. *Pencil Sketches of Colorado.* Denver: 1866.

Miles, Nelson A. *Personal Recollections.* Chicago and New York: 1896.

New York Illustrated News. October 4, 1862.

"No Name." *Denver Dan Jr., and His Band of Dead Shots.* New York: September 25, 1896.

Official Guide of Chicago, Kansas City and Denver Short Line. February, 1875.

O'Ryan, William, Rev., and Malone, Thomas H., Rev. *History of the Catholic Church in Colorado.* Denver: 1889.

Richardson, Albert D. *Beyond the Mississippi.* Hartford: 1867.

Richardson, Leander P. *No Slouch. A Romance of Pike's Peak.* New York: May 29, 1890.

Rideing, William H. *Boys in the Mountains and on the Plains.* New York: 1882.

Rocky Mountain News. 1890-1898.

Rocky Mountain Official Railway Guide. Denver: November, 1894.

Rocky Mountain Official Railway Guide. Denver: April,
1896; November, 1897.

Rusling, Gen. James T. *Across America.* New York: 1874.

Scribner's Magazine. New York: 1871-72-76-78-79; 1881, 1901.

"Cheyenne Sketchbook (captured at Summit Springs, July 11, 1869)." Western Collection, Colorado State Historical Society.

Smart, Stephen F. *Leadville, Ten Mile, Eagle River. . . .* Kansas City, Missouri: 1879.

Smiley, Jerome C. *History of Denver.* Denver: 1903.

Souvenir des Denver Turnvereins. Denver: 1890.

State Business Directory of Colorado. Denver: 1881.

Strahorn, Robert E. *To the Rockies and Beyond.* Omaha: 1879.

Sweetser, Moses F. *King's Handbook of the United States.* Buffalo: 1890.

Tenney, E. P. *Colorado and Homes in the New West.* Boston: 1880.

Thayer, William M. *Marvels of the New West.* Norwich, Connecticut: 1887.

The Aldine: The Art Journal of America. New York: February, 1873.

The Illustrated Miners' Hand-Book and Guide to Pike's Peak. Saint Louis: 1859.

Tice, John H. *Over the Plains.* St. Louis: 1872.

Twitchell, Ralph Emerson. *The Spanish Archives of New Mexico.* Cedar Rapids, Iowa: 1914.

Union Pacific Railroad Company. *Union Pacific Sketch Book.* Omaha: 1887.

Vivian, A. Pendarves. *Wanderings in the Western Land.* London: 1880.

Wallihan, Samuel S. and Bigney, T. O. *The Rocky Mountain Directory and Colorado Gazetteer for 1871.* Denver: 1870.

Ware, Eugene Fitch. *The Indian War of 1864.* Topeka: 1911.

Western Collection, Colorado State Historical Society.

Western Collection, Denver Public Library.

Wharton, J. E. *History of the City of Denver from the Earliest Settlement to the Present Time.* Denver: 1866.

Whitney, J. P. *Colorado, In the United States of America.* London: 1867.

Williams, Henry L. *The Picturesque West.* New York: 1891.

Wood, Stanley. *Over the Range to the Golden Gate.* Chicago: 1889.

INDEX